God is always present. That's especially
important to remember during the
silences when you may not
sense his presence.

Presented To

_____

Presented By

_____

Date

_____

When you schedule your life according to God's wisdom, you will find greater contentment in what you do.

# SIMPLE LIVING™

## for Teens

# SIMPLE LIVING

## for Teens

God's Guide to Enjoying What Matters Most

inspirio

*Simple Living for Teens*
ISBN 0-310-80348-9

Copyright © 2004 by GRQ Ink, Inc.
Franklin, Tennessee 37067
"Simple Living" is a trademark owned by GRQ, Inc.

Published by Inspirio™, The gift group of Zondervan
5300 Patterson Avenue, SE
Grand Rapids, Michigan 49530

Requests for information should be addressed to:
Inspirio™, The gift group of Zondervan
Grand Rapids, Michigan 49530
http://www.inspiriogifts.com

Compiler: Lila Empson
Associate Editor: Janice Jacobson
Project Manager: Tom Dean
Manuscript written by Jonathan Rogers
Design: Whisner Design Group, Tulsa, Oklahoma

Printed in China.

03 04 05/HK/ 4 3 2 1

We need to find God, and he cannot be found in noise and restlessness. God is the friend of silence. See how nature—trees, flowers, grass—grows in silence; see the stars, the moon and the sun, how they move in silence . . . We need silence to be able to touch souls.

MOTHER TERESA

Paul wrote: "Am I now trying to get people to think well of me? Or do I want God to think well of me? Am I trying to please people? If I were, I would not be serving Christ."

GALATIANS 1:10 NIrV

# Table of Contents

# Introduction

Life is complex, and time seems to spin by faster each day. You're tired of feeling squeezed by demands and pressured to go even faster. And you wonder, *Is it possible to live a simpler, less hurried life?*

Absolutely—and you can start right now.

Here, forty thoughtful meditations reveal how you can discover God's gift of inner peace and soul-soothing serenity. So set aside some time just for you, sit down with this book, and consider your options for embracing the simple life you dream about.

Rest is not idleness, and to lie sometimes on the grass on a summer day listening to the murmur of water, or watching the clouds float across the sky, is hardly a waste of time.

SIR JOHN LUBBOCK

# Beyond Words

Jesus said, "When you pray, do not use a lot of meaningless words."
Matthew 6:7 GNT

Have you made your prayer life more complicated than it should be? That's not at all unusual. The more you read and hear about the importance of prayer, the more complex your prayers are likely to become. This is especially true if you are self-conscious when you pray in public, but it's also true in your private prayer time, when an excess of words can prevent you from listening to God. Maybe it's time to learn a new way of praying, one that will enrich your relationship with God and ease your discomfort with praying in public.

You start by paring down your "many words," gradually learning to spend more time listening to God than talking to him. God does not need to hear your words as much as he desires to hear your heart. Sitting silently in his presence, focusing all of your attention on him, allowing your thoughts to go where your heart leads, you discover that he begins to sort out the jumble in your head.

Imagine Jesus praying all night alone in the mountains, away from the crowds—or set apart from his disciples in the Garden of Gethsemane. A few of the words he spoke to his Father in the garden are recorded in Scripture, and he most likely spoke other words that no one heard. He probably experienced periods of silence, allowing God the Father to speak to him. Likewise when you pray, God is active during those silent periods, beginning the work in your life that your prayer was intended to accomplish in the first place.

As you learn to use fewer words when you pray, you become more comfortable with those times of silence, and eventually you begin to welcome them. After a while, you will see how few your genuine needs and desires are as well. By being still and tuning out the clamor of the culture and the confusion in your own mind, you will finally be in a position to hear the whisperings of God. Moreover, his whisperings will always bring clarity to your life—never complication.

## One Final Thought

Let your life become a prayer to God by choosing to lavish him with your attention rather than with many words.

# Thoughts for Simply Living

O LORD, I call to you; come quickly to me. Hear my voice when I call to you. May my prayer be set before you like incense; may the lifting up of my hands be like the evening sacrifice. Set a guard over my mouth, O LORD; keep watch over the door of my lips.

> PSALM 141:1–3 NIV

The fewer words the better the prayer.

> MARTIN LUTHER

Think before you speak, and don't make any rash promises to God. He is in heaven and you are on earth, so don't say any more than you have to.

> ECCLESIASTES 5:2 GNT

Whenever the sounds of the world die out in the soul, or sink low, then we hear the whisperings of God.

> FREDERICK W. FABER

# Remember...

_____Your prayers are an offering to God. Give serious thought to what it is that you are actually giving him.

_____When you become absorbed in God, you lose the self-consciousness that hinders your genuine communication with him.

_____God is always present. That's especially important to remember during the silences when you may not sense his presence.

_____When you think of your life as a living prayer to God, your times of conscious prayer, whether vocal or silent, flow from a heart already turned toward him.

# Simplify...

Write your prayers in longhand. If your hand gets tired, you may be using too many words.

Sit silently and focus on God for several minutes. Gradually increase your silent time.

When you're stuck, find an appropriate prayer in the Bible and pray it to God.

Find a prayer partner who will help you keep your prayer life focused.

Establish a daily prayer routine that you believe you will be able to follow.

_In prayer it is better to have a heart without words,_
_than words without a heart._

JOHN BUNYAN

# Where Does Your Money Go?

The LORD said, "Why spend money on what is not bread, and your labor on what does not satisfy? Listen, listen to me, and eat what is good, and your soul will delight in the richest of fare."

Isaiah 55:2 NIV

If you're like many teens, you spend your week juggling school, extracurricular activities, church—and doing what you can to earn some extra money. Whether your money comes from your allowance, occasional baby-sitting or lawn-mowing jobs, or part-time work, having your own money gives you a feeling of independence and helps you learn to handle money responsibly. You probably already realize that if you're not careful, you can easily waste your money on things that bring you no lasting satisfaction—things that complicate your life and you end up stuck with so much that you really don't need.

So how do you determine where your money goes? You may feel free to spend your money on whatever you like. People who create TV commercials, magazine advertisements, and pop-up ads on the Internet, of course, want to help you exercise that freedom by telling you what you must buy to be truly happy. Meanwhile God—who gave you freedom in the first place—has provided written guidelines on how to use money in a way that genuinely satisfies.

Look at the contrast: Advertisers tell you that you deserve a break today; you work hard for your money, and you have the right to shop till you drop. But God says your soul will never be satisfied with the things you buy; contentment with what you have frees you from the love of money and keeps your financial life focused and uncomplicated. God wants your soul to delight in the "richest of fare"—the spiritual treasure Jesus speaks of in Matthew 6. That means doing what God has called you to do. When you invest in the things of God, your money takes on eternal value—something advertisers cannot promise or deliver.

When you begin to ignore advertising claims that equate spending with happiness, you take a major step toward learning to handle your money responsibly. The next time you are tempted to buy something you don't need—whether it's a mega-sized order of fries or yet another DVD—think about where that desire came from and trust the one who wants to see your soul delight in spiritual treasure.

## One Final Thought

Finding contentment in what you already have is the essence of simple living.

# Thoughts for Simply Living

Jesus said, "Do not store up for yourselves treasures on earth, where moth and rust destroy, and where thieves break in and steal. But store up for yourselves treasures in heaven, where moth and rust do not destroy, and where thieves do not break in and steal. For where your treasure is, there your heart will be also."

MATTHEW 6:19–21 NIV

Money spent on myself may be a millstone about my neck; money spent on others may give me wings like the angels.

ROSWELL DWIGHT HITCHCOCK

Keep your lives free from the love of money and be content with what you have, because God has said, "Never will I leave you; never will I forsake you."

HEBREWS 13:5 NIV

Unnecessary possessions are unnecessary burdens. If you have them, you will have to take care of them.

PEACE PILGRIM

# Remember...

_____Learning to handle money God's way frees you from the desire to accumulate things that tend to complicate your life.

_____Investing in the kingdom of God gives your money eternal value.

_____You can be content with what you have when what you have includes a personal relationship with Jesus Christ.

_____God wants your soul to delight in the kind of spiritual treasure that money cannot buy.

# Simplify...

Pray about what God would have you do with your money.

Before you make a purchase, ask yourself if that purchase will complicate or simplify your life.

Learn to identify the subtle and not-so-subtle ways some advertisements try to manipulate your spending.

Jesus had much to say about money. See what you can learn from his teachings on money in the Gospels.

Ask God to make you aware of what brings genuine satisfaction to your life.

*While there is flesh there is money—or the want of money.*

SAMUEL BUTLER

19

# Refreshing Your Body, Mind, and Spirit

The LORD grants sleep to those he loves.
Psalm 127:2 NIV

Do you ever feel as if you get enough sleep? Probably most people would answer a resounding no to that question. Your very full and active life leaves little time for sleep or genuine rest. But God created your body and your spirit in such a way that he made rest an essential part of life. Your body—and your spirit—can only go just so long without an extended break from activity. It's amazing how much simpler the problems and challenges in your life can seem when you've had the right amount of sleep.

Getting the rest you need can be difficult. As always, though, God is there to help you meet that challenge. Because God loves you he provides sleep so you can become rejuvenated and more productive in your schoolwork or your job, eliminating the need to put in long (and often unproductive) hours. Jesus offers to walk beside you and share your burden as you go through your day. Then when it's time to go to sleep after a full and active day, God stays awake and watches over you so you may sleep peacefully, knowing everything is under his control.

When you trust God to give you the rest you need, your energy level increases, your mind becomes sharper, and your spirit is freshened, making it easier to place other areas of your life under his care. Problems that seemed monumental when you were plagued by fatigue shrink to a manageable size; what once appeared to be a complex issue now seems comparatively simple, all because you allowed God to restore your physical, mental, and spiritual energy through rest, relaxation, and sound sleep.

Your schoolwork will get done. Your time at work or doing chores will be productive. You will be able to join in other activities and have some fun. Allow God to give you the rest you need. Don't try to do it all on your own; allow Jesus to share your burden. As you fall asleep at night, God remains wide awake so you can enjoy peaceful slumber.

## One Final Thought

When you allow God to refresh you, you are better able to meet the challenges of each day.

# Thoughts for Simply Living

Jesus said, "Take my yoke upon you and learn from me, for I am gentle and humble in heart, and you will find rest for your souls."

MATTHEW 11:29 NIV

Every now and then go away, have a little relaxation, for when you come back to your work your judgment will be surer.

LEONARDO DA VINCI

The LORD will watch over your coming and going both now and forevermore.

PSALM 121:8 NIV

Rest is not idleness, and to lie sometimes on the grass on a summer day listening to the murmur of water, or watching the clouds float across the sky, is hardly a waste of time.

SIR JOHN LUBBOCK

# Remember...

Rest and relaxation help simplify your life by enabling you to keep complicated problems in perspective.

The peaceful sleep God provides will rejuvenate your body, mind, and spirit.

Jesus wants to share your burdens throughout the day so you can be unburdened when it's time to sleep.

Fatigue can make you unproductive; you need rest to make your waking hours more productive.

## Simplify...

Experiment with your sleep pattern. A twenty-minute nap after school may make you sharper at work or when doing your homework.

Before you go to bed, list what you need to do the next day, then give the list to God and forget it.

Read the Bible or a devotional book to prepare your mind and spirit for a good night's sleep.

When you begin to tire during the day, health experts suggest getting fresh air, taking a walk, or drinking water.

Talk to God as you get ready to go to sleep.

*Day begins not at dawn but at dusk, with God's long night of work within us as we rest.*

EUGENE PETERSON

# The Plain and Simple Truth

You were taught to start living a new life . . . So each of you must get rid of your lying. Speak the truth to your neighbor.

Ephesians 4:24–25 NIrV

If you've ever told a whopper of a lie, you already know how quickly dishonesty can complicate your life. You had to work extra hard to cover up, remember exactly what you said, maybe even get someone else all tangled up in your deception by asking her to go along with your lie. What a mess! It may be hard to face the consequences of telling the truth, but it sure makes your life a lot simpler when you do. When you own up to the truth, your clear, uncluttered conscience lets you get on with your life. Furthermore, you keep your life simple by avoiding the need to cover up for a lie or to keep your stories straight.

God places a high value on honesty, and he wants his people to do the same. God knows how easily lying can become a habit that destroys your integrity and damages your relationships with God and with other people. The many Bible verses and stories about lies and deception reveal how severe the consequences of dishonesty are. They are always more severe than the consequences of telling the truth.

When you make it a habit to tell the truth, you simplify your life. You also keep the line of communication open with God. You can approach him without that nagging sense of guilt that results when you've been dishonest. The same holds true with other people. Just think how much less complicated your relationships are—whether it's with your parents, your friends, or even your teachers—when you've been completely honest with them.

Keep your life uncomplicated by resolving always to tell the plain and simple truth. Show respect for God and for others by always being honest with them. When you begin to acquire a reputation as an honest person—a person whose word can be trusted—you bring honor to God, your family, and yourself. In return, you will enjoy the blessings of a clear conscience, right relationships, and freedom from the need to keep your stories straight.

## One Final Thought

Lies tend to create the need for more lies.
That's a complication you don't need!

# Thoughts for Simply Living

The tongue that brings healing is a tree of life, but a deceitful tongue crushes the spirit.

PROVERBS 15:4 NIV

We lie loudest when we lie to ourselves.

ERIC HOFFER

Truthful words last forever. But lies last for only a moment. There are lies in the hearts of those who plan evil. But there is joy for those who work to bring peace. No harm comes to godly people. But sinners have all the trouble they can handle. The LORD hates those whose lips tell lies, but he is pleased with people who tell the truth.

PROVERBS 12:19–22 NIrV

The essence of lying is in deception, not in words.

JOHN RUSKIN

# Remember...

_____God wants you to place as high a value on honesty as he does.

_____You can trust God to be with you when you tell the truth, even if your honesty results in difficult consequences.

_____Honesty in your relationships keeps the lines of communication open.

_____You show respect for God and for other people whenever you are truthful with them.

# Simplify...

Look through the book of Proverbs and take note of what it has to say about honesty.

Ask a friend to hold you accountable by regularly asking you how honest you've been.

Memorize Job 27:3–4 and quote it to yourself when you're tempted to lie.

Everyone struggles with being honest in some areas of life. Identify yours, and journal about ways you can meet that challenge.

Pray that God's Spirit would give you the desire and power to tell the truth so you can have a clear conscience.

*An honest person is the noblest work of God.*

ALEXANDER POPE

# The Lure of "Easy" Credit

Let no debt remain outstanding, except the continuing debt to love one another.
Romans 13:8 NIV

At this point in your life, it's unlikely that you have a serious problem with debt. But in the coming years, you will be flooded with credit card offers. Credit card companies will try to convince you that you can have it all—now—thanks to the convenience of buying on credit. They make it sound so easy, but few things can complicate your life quite as quickly as debt can.

Simply put, debt is a loan against the promise—but not the certainty—of future income. That tends to complicate the financial picture a bit, because when payday rolls around, there are lots of other places your money needs to go. But now you have to factor in the payment on the debt you owe. And life really gets thorny when there's suddenly no paycheck, yet you're still expected to make your payments as usual.

From the very beginning, God counseled the Israelites to avoid becoming indebted to others, and he repeated this counsel to the early church. God wants his people to serve him alone, and he knows that when his people are in debt, they become servants to those who lend.

Would you want to serve anyone but God? But the moment you take on debt, you become subservient to the lender. Interest on the debt you owe causes you to spend much more than the original item or service is worth, which is bad stewardship. What's worse, as a minor you place your parents under the burden of your debt, compounding the problem and threatening to damage your family relationships. When you come of age, credit card companies anticipate that your parents will still pay up (even though your parents aren't legally required to do so) in order to protect your credit rating.

Debt may be an easy thing to get into, but there's nothing simple about getting out of it. Being in debt is a complication you need to avoid. That means you will not always be able to have what you want. However, it also means that you will avoid many things you don't want; starting with a strained relationship with God and your parents and the pressure to make monthly payments. Resolve to stay out of debt and retain your ability to spend money wisely; that's one resolution you will never regret making.

## One Final Thought

Keep yourself free of subservience to anyone but the Lord.

# Thoughts for Simply Living

Paul wrote: "I have received full payment and even more;
I am amply supplied . . . And my God will meet all your
needs according to his glorious riches in Christ Jesus.
To our God and Father be glory for ever and ever."

PHILIPPIANS 4:18–20 NIV

Debt is the worst poverty.

THOMAS FULLER

The rich rule over the poor, and the borrower is servant to
the lender.

PROVERBS 22:7 NIV

Annual income twenty pounds, annual expenditure nineteen pounds six, result
happiness. Annual income twenty pounds, annual expenditure twenty pounds
ought and six, result misery.

CHARLES DICKENS

# Remember...

_____Freedom from debt gives you greater freedom to spend your money wisely.

_____God wants to keep you free from becoming financially indebted to others.

_____Living within your means keeps your financial life simple.

_____Serving God brings joy; serving creditors brings misery.

# Simplify...

At this point in your life, say no to credit card offers and "easy-payment" plans.

Talk to your friends about sharing the cost of a high-ticket item that all of you need.

Search the Web for articles on teen debt, such as those from Crown Financial Ministries (www.crown.org; click on Library).

Ask God to give you the faith to believe that he will provide your needs.

Become knowledgeable now about such things as interest rates, so you will be prepared to make wise decisions later on.

_Most people would be happy to pay as they go, if only they could catch up on where they have been._

JOHN C. MAXWELL

# Simple Living
## Everyday Simplicity

Simplicity is making the journey of life with just enough baggage.

CHARLES WARNER

Jesus said, "The thief comes only to steal and kill and destroy; I came that they may have life, and have it abundantly."

JOHN 10:10 NASB

If the Son makes you free, you will be free indeed.

JOHN 8:36 NASB

The LORD is my shepherd, I have everything I need.

PSALM 23:1 GNT

Simplicity is freedom—

Freedom from the restless urge to accumulate,

Freedom from the slavish need to please everybody,

Freedom to do what's best.


Simplicity is abundance—

The overflow of a spirit released

From the compulsion to do more, to get more...

A spirit released to be more.

BARBARA E. BRIM

# What's Best for You

Jesus said, "Come to me, all you who are weary and burdened, and I will give you rest."

Matthew 11:28 NIV

*Stop the World—I Want to Get Off* was the title of a popular musical years ago, and it may also express the way you feel right now. You've got school, a job, sports, church, family, friends, and maybe a pet or two, all vying for your time. Add to that homework, devotions, fund-raising, club meetings, volunteer work, and—*whew!* It's no wonder you want to get off and let the world spin a time or two without you!

If you feel this way, it probably is time to stop. Not the world, of course, but the flurry of activity that has become your life. God wants you to enjoy life to the fullest and find contentment, but you can't exactly do that when every minute is full of obligations, no matter how enjoyable some of your obligations may be. In fact, God created and set apart an entire day solely for a break from the routine obligations of life.

Once you understand what it means to have a simple

lifestyle and start making it your own, you'll want to apply it to your schedule. You can enjoy good results right away. Think carefully about all of the activities that you are involved in, and ask God to show you which ones you can let go of. He'll help you by giving you the wisdom and discernment to determine how to prioritize your many commitments.

Remember, too, that many of the things you're involved in may not be "commitments" in the true sense of the word. If you have promised to baby-sit for a neighbor every Tuesday night so she can attend night school, that's a genuine commitment. But attending after-school meetings of the history club may not be, unless you are an officer or the group is counting on you to fulfill a commitment you've made to them.

One thing is certain: the world won't stop for you. But you can stop—right now—and ask God to show you the unnecessary activities you're involved in. Let him help you pare them down to what he knows is best for you.

## One Final Thought

When you restrict your activities to what you know is God's will for you, you automatically simplify your life.

# Thoughts for Simply Living

[Martha] had a sister called Mary, who sat at the Lord's feet listening to what he said. But Martha was distracted by all the preparations that had to be made. She came to him and asked, "Lord, don't you care that my sister has left me to do the work by myself? Tell her to help me!" "Martha, Martha," the Lord answered, "you are worried and upset about many things, but only one thing is needed. Mary has chosen what is better, and it will not be taken away from her."

LUKE 10:39–42 NIV

God requires a faithful fulfillment of the merest trifle given us to do, rather than the most ardent aspiration to things to which we are not called.

SAINT FRANCIS DE SALES

Paul wrote: "Am I now trying to get people to think well of me? Or do I want God to think well of me? Am I trying to please people? If I were, I would not be serving Christ."

GALATIANS 1:10 NIrV

There is time enough for everything in the course of the day if you do but one thing once; but there is not time enough in the year if you do two things at a time.

LORD CHESTERFIELD

## Remember...

_____When you schedule your life according to God's wisdom, you will find greater contentment in what you do.

_____Letting go of unnecessary activities can bring peace and structure to a chaotic lifestyle.

_____God wants you to enjoy life and gave you the gift of the seventh day to take a break from obligations.

_____Mary chose "what is better" (Luke 10:42 NIV)—attentiveness to the Lord over unceasing activity.

## Simplify...

List every activity you are involved in and pray over each item on the list, asking God if you should eliminate any.

Make a habit of consulting with God before you take on any more commitments.

Determine if any of your commitments indicate a lack of trust in the Lord.

Are you a people-pleaser? Simplify your life by becoming a God-pleaser.

Allow Jesus to carry your burdens for you.

_If you have so much business to attend to that you have no time to pray, depend upon it that you have more business on hand than God ever intended you should have._

DWIGHT L. MOODY

# Substance Over Style

Jesus said, "Why do you worry about clothes? See how the lilies of the field grow. They do not labor or spin. Yet I tell you that not even Solomon in all his splendor was dressed like one of these . . . But seek first his kingdom and his righteousness, and all these things will be given to you as well."

Matthew 6:28–29, 33 NIV

If you take an honest look at your closet, you will probably find clothes you don't wear anymore. Some may no longer fit; others may require more care than you have time to give them. What was in last year is out this year, and what you thought looked good in the store—thanks to a cool-looking mannequin and even cooler-looking cashier—doesn't look so cool after all. You end up with a closet full of clothes but few you can wear.

If you are serious about simplifying your life, your closet is a good place to get started. But you are going to have to be ruthless. That means getting rid of every piece of clothing that doesn't fit, isn't in style, and no longer suits your taste. Most people tend to wear the same few items of clothing over and over again, and those are the ones you want to make sure you save. With just those few items plus several special-occasion pieces, you will have a manageable wardrobe that emphasizes practical substance over impractical style.

In time, you will realize the freedom that comes from limiting the size of your wardrobe. Having to make too many choices can be unnerving, whether those choices involve everyday issues like what to wear or long-term issues like the best career for you. When you reduce the number of decisions you have to make in the less important areas of your life, you clear your mind to focus on more important issues, like your relationship with the Lord and the direction your life is taking. The decisions that affect those larger issues are the ones worth spending your time on.

Who you are on the inside is more important than what you wear on the outside. Rearrange your priorities so you are focusing on things of lasting value, like how to deepen your spiritual life, the steps you can take to improve your relationships, and what you can do to overcome that annoying habit you have, whatever it may be. Making sound decisions in those areas of your life will never go out of style.

## One Final Thought

The kind of clothes you wear will never be as significant
as the kind of person you are.

# Thoughts for Simply Living

Jesus said to his disciples, "I tell you, do not worry about your life, what you will eat; or about your body, what you will wear. Life is more than food, and the body more than clothes."

LUKE 12:22–23 NIV

Do not conceive that fine clothes make fine men, any more than fine feathers make fine birds.

GEORGE WASHINGTON

We brought nothing into the world, and we can take nothing out of it. But if we have food and clothing, we will be content with that.

1 TIMOTHY 6:7–8 NIV

I never thought that a lot of money or fine clothes—the finer things of life—would make you happy. My concept of happiness is to be filled in a spiritual sense.

CORETTA SCOTT KING

# Remember...

_____Your self-esteem should be closely tied with who you are in Christ and not with what you wear.

_____Any time you reduce the number of things you must maintain, you free up time for the important things in life.

_____By focusing on things of lasting value, you can make changes where they count—on the inside.

_____A spirit of gratitude toward God adds blessing to what you do have.

# Simplify...

Get rid of every piece of clothing that no longer fits or that you no longer wear.

Donate all your unwanted clothes to charity.

Learn the right way to launder your clothes in order to prolong their life.

Swap clothes with a friend (check with your parents for permission first).

When you must buy new, avoid clothes requiring time-consuming or expensive care, like dry cleaning.

*Fashions are always changing, but the person with style is never out of date.*

BAER'S ALMANAC

41

# Preventive Maintenance

Don't you know that your body is the temple of the Holy Spirit, who lives in you and who was given to you by God?

1 Corinthians 6:19 GNT

Have you ever noticed how much time your parents spend on maintaining your home? Even if you live in an apartment, your parents still have things to maintain, like appliances. From an annual checkup of the heating system to removing the lint from the dryer after each use, regular maintenance wards off problems later on. The same principle of preventive maintenance applies to a much more serious issue as well: your health.

You may not have given much thought to practicing preventive maintenance when it comes to your health; you're young, you're probably in relatively good shape, and you probably seldom need to see a doctor. In fact, unless a chronic physical problem has sidelined you, you may not think about your health very much at all.

You do need to give your health some thought and attention, though. Look at it this way: You may live in a half dozen or more houses in your lifetime, but you have only one body to last you that same amount of time. What's more, as a Christian your body is considered to be the temple of God's Spirit, and you should treat it with corresponding respect. With God's Spirit dwelling within you, you have an added incentive to take care of your body.

Your health is an important issue with God. Physical problems that could have been avoided with a little maintenance complicate your life and interfere with your ability to serve God. It's much wiser to exercise, eat right, and floss now than to undergo cardiac surgery, a weight-loss regimen, and a root canal later on. When you take care of your health, you show God that you appreciate the life he has given you.

Take time to assess what you're doing to maintain your health at this point in your life. Are you getting enough fresh air, walking instead of driving or riding, and eating regular, balanced meals? Sounds like what you'd hear in health class, doesn't it? But your physical well-being can affect both your emotional health and spiritual usefulness. Simple living often means taking the long view—doing things now to avoid complicating your life later on—especially when it comes to your health.

## One Final Thought

When you are physically healthy, you are likely to have more energy to serve God and others.

# Thoughts for Simply Living

Don't you know that you yourselves are God's temple and
that God's Spirit lives in you? If anyone destroys God's
temple, God will destroy him; for God's temple is sacred,
and you are that temple.

1 CORINTHIANS 3:16 NIV

Look to your health; and if you have it, praise God, and value it next to a good
conscience; for health is the second blessing that we mortals are capable of; a
blessing that money cannot buy.

IZAAK WALTON

You were washed, you were sanctified, you were justified in
the name of the Lord Jesus Christ and by the Spirit of our
God. "Everything is permissible for me"—but not everything
is beneficial. "Everything is permissible for me"—but I will
not be mastered by anything . . . You were bought at a price.
Therefore honor God with your body.

1 CORINTHIANS 6:11–12, 20 NIV

Health can be squandered, but not stored up.

MASON COOLEY

# Remember...

_____As in other areas of your life, the healthful things you do today will have long-term, positive consequences.

_____One way to show your gratitude to God for the life he has given you is to take care of your health.

_____Serving God involves your entire being—body, mind and spirit.

_____You honor God with your body by being careful about the way you treat it.

# Simplify...

Ask God to help you identify those health issues you need to take care of first.

Recruit a friend to walk or run with you on a regular basis.

Stock up on healthful snacks like baby carrots so you won't be tempted to rely on fast food.

Make a list of things you could be doing on a daily, weekly, and monthly basis to maintain your health. Remember that prevention is simpler than the cure.

Get moving! Find an upbeat music CD that you can exercise to.

*There is no exercise better for the heart than reaching down and lifting people up.*

JOHN ANDREW HOLMES

# Too Much for One Person

Everything should be done in a fitting and orderly way.
1 Corinthians 14:40 NIV

Stuff. It's everywhere, isn't it? In any given month, you probably accumulate more stuff than you want or need—like magazines you never have time to read, the pack of socks your mother bought for you by mistake, mail from college and military recruiters, and flyers from companies hawking school-related merchandise. Add that to what you've already accumulated, and you end up with the opposite of simplicity: clutter.

There's a reason—actually, several reasons—why the Bible advocates orderliness. First, creation itself was the result of God bringing order to chaos so people would have an orderly world in which to live. Second, God is god of order, not confusion. And third, God does not like excess.

Clutter creates a confused environment. Moreover, clutter reflects excess. If you have so much stuff that it clutters your room, you probably have too much stuff for one person. Some people coexist with clutter better than others do. Even if the stuff around you doesn't bother you right now, eventually you will have to deal with it—and by then, you will have a massive project to undertake. The time to start to bring order to the chaos around you is now, before it gets any worse.

You need to make wise decisions about the excess stuff in your life. It's not enough simply to throw out the excess; your goal should be to recycle what you no longer need, thus avoiding contributing to the county landfill. That old 386 computer can go to a school that teaches keyboarding skills to kids in poverty-stricken areas. An analog cell phone can go to a shelter and be refurbished and given to battered women for emergency use. Much of what you have can go to some kind of charity or nonprofit institution like a school or library.

As you cut down on clutter, ask God to give you a greater awareness of just how little you need and how much simpler your life would be without so much stuff. Once you get rid of the excess, you may discover that having less stuff translates into a more fulfilling life.

## One Final Thought

The more stuff you have, the more you have to take care of; the less stuff you have, the more time you have to truly enjoy the life God has given you.

# Thoughts for Simply Living

[There is] a time to keep and a time to throw away.
ECCLESIASTES 3:6 NIV

We are the slaves of objects around us.
JOHANN WOLFGANG VON GOETHE

As goods increase, so do those who consume them. And what benefit are they to the owner except to feast his eyes on them?
ECCLESIASTES 5:11 NIV

Half of the secular unrest and dismal, profane sadness of modern society . . . comes from the greedy notion that a man's life does consist, after all, in the abundance of things that he possesseth, and that it is, somehow or other, more respectable and pious to be always at work trying to make a larger living, than it is to lie on your back in the green pastures and beside the still waters, and thank God that you are alive.
HENRY VAN DYKE

# Remember...

_____Your excess stuff can be a blessing to those who have little.

_____God brought order to the pre-creation chaos, knowing that humans function best in an orderly environment.

_____God has made you the caretaker of all that you have, and he wants you to take that responsibility seriously.

_____Material clutter creates a complicated lifestyle rather than a simple one.

# Simplify...

Reduce the clutter around you by passing on to others what you no longer need.

> Fight clutter by resisting the urge to accumulate more stuff.

Keep a list of charities and institutions to which you can donate your excess.

> Ask God to help you make wise decisions about dealing with what you have—and want to have.

Try to find a new home or a new use for your discards rather than throwing them away.

*Straighten up your room first, then the world.*

JEFF JORDAN

49

# The High Cost of Status

Wise people act in keeping with the knowledge they have. But foolish people show how foolish they are.

Proverbs 13:16 NIrV

Car maintenance? What does that have to do with simple living for teenagers? A lot, because even if you don't own a car yet, you will eventually. The kind of car you buy, and the degree of maintenance it requires, can make a big difference when it comes to a lifestyle of simplicity.

The Bible, of course, doesn't mention cars. But it says a great deal about the way you spend your time and your money—and the way you indulge in worldly pursuits. Like nothing else, the kind of car a teen drives can represent his or her indulgence in worldly pursuits—because to some people a really cool car represents the ultimate teenage status symbol.

That status symbol, though, comes at a steep price. The cooler the car, the more costly it may be to buy, maintain, and insure, and the more likely it is to be stolen or "keyed." Its owner easily becomes its slave, worrying over every little sound and every little scratch that might make it somewhat less than cool.

But could a car—even a "cool" one—possibly be a sign of your status in God's eyes? You know the answer to that one. So, that being the case, it makes little sense to burden yourself with unnecessary expense and excessive upkeep of more car than you need. A car suited to your needs and your budget contributes to your well-being; anything else is a drain on your time and energy and serves to complicate rather than simplify your life.

Living a life of simplicity often requires reordering the way you think about things, and that can mean viewing things in terms of their basic purpose. Learn to think of a car as a means of getting from here to there—basic transportation. Others may complicate their lives with their costly status symbols, but you don't have to. Your commitment to a simplified lifestyle means that your less flashy but more reliable car will give you fewer headaches and more time to enjoy the one life God has given you.

## One Final Thought

God wants you to give careful thought to the way you spend your time and your money.

# Thoughts for Simply Living

A man in the crowd said to Jesus, "Teacher, tell my brother to divide with me the property our father left us." Jesus answered him, "Friend, who gave me the right to judge or to divide the property between you two?" And he went on to say to them all, "Watch out and guard yourselves from every kind of greed; because your true life is not made up of the things you own, no matter how rich you may be."

LUKE 12:13–15 GNT

Fifty years from now, it will not matter what kind of car you drove.

AUTHOR UNKNOWN

[The grace of God] teaches us to say "No" to ungodliness and worldly passions, and to live self-controlled, upright and godly lives in this present age.

TITUS 2:12 NIV

We are the first nation in the history of the world to go to the poorhouse in an automobile.

WILL ROGERS

# Remember...

_____Low-maintenance items help free your life of unnecessary complications.

_____The ultimate symbol of your status is the cross of Jesus Christ, not your material possessions.

_____Simple living often involves restructuring the way you think about things.

_____Your money and your time are valuable; make wise use of both.

# Simplify...

Consider the cost of maintenance in time and money when you buy anything, but especially a high-ticket item like a car.

Give your time to others rather than to things.

Pray about every major purchase you make.

Avoid status symbols; they complicate rather than simplify your life.

Learn to think of things in terms of their basic purpose.

_I was just thinking how much you can tell about a person from such simple things. Your car, for instance._

A. I. BEZZERIDES

# Simple Living
## Spiritual Energy

*Teach us to count our days that we may gain a wise heart.*

PSALM 90:12 NRSV

A lost inch of gold may be reclaimed, but never a lost inch of time.

ANCIENT PROVERB

*There is a time for everything, and a season for every activity under heaven.*

ECCLESIASTES 3:1 NIV

*Show me, O LORD, my life's end and the number of my days; let me know how fleeting is my life.*

PSALM 39:4 NIV

Though I was made for eternity,

My life is measured out in minutes, days, years.

Each second is a gift from God,

Each hour is in His hands.

God, grant that I might use these gifts,

And not discard them like so many broken toys.

God, give me grace that I might own my time

And not be owned by circumstance.

Deliver me from things that steal my days—

The sloth, the worry, the urgent trifle,

The careless waste of hours

On things that cannot satisfy—

So that I might glorify You, serve others,

And be fitted for eternity,

Where I'll be freed from time.

CARLA SCHULTZ

# A Second Wind from God

Those who hope in the LORD will renew their strength.

Isaiah 40:31 NIV

Have you ever prayed for something for so long that you felt as if you were running a marathon? You're totally energized at first and refreshed along the way like a runner whose thirst is quenched by periodic sips of cool water. But at some point you hit the proverbial wall, the place that marathon runners describe as the make-or-break point. Fail to push through the wall and the race is lost; make it through, and the finish line is as good as yours. You made it through!

Unlike a marathon runner, you don't need to rely on your own willpower and strength to push through the spiritual wall you're facing. The key to making it through is handing over your faith to the one who promises to strengthen and encourage you. Trying to break through in your own strength is pointless; God wants you to forget yourself and remember him, along with every promise he has made to see you through. He wants you to give it up—

not your faith in him, but your faith in your own ability to endure.

"Spiritual striving"—the intense and unnecessary effort you make to please God and grow as a believer—wastes energy and turns simple faith into a complicated and often rigid set of religious activities. The resulting fatigue makes any wall you face seem insurmountable. Striving can also deceive you into thinking that the answer to your prayer depends on you—you must pray harder, fast longer, read more Scripture. Unless God has clearly led you to do those things, you are placing your faith in your activities instead of God. He alone can provide the second wind you need to keep believing.

Give your striving to God. Write down your requests, your concerns, your hopes—and consciously give them to God. Trust him to provide the answer in his time and his way. Patiently await the answer, but keep your focus on God and your relationship with him. He promises to renew your strength when you feel your faith begin to falter. When God renews your strength, you can have confidence that you will make it to the finish line.

# One Final Thought

God's second wind provides all the spiritual energy you need to keep believing that he will answer your prayers.

# Thoughts for Simply Living

Do not fear, for I am with you; do not be dismayed, for I am your God. I will strengthen you and help you; I will uphold you with my righteous right hand.

ISAIAH 41:10 NIV

Surrender refreshes and regenerates. Failure to surrender strains and wearies.

PIERO FERRUCCI

Do not throw away your confidence; it will be richly rewarded. You need to persevere so that when you have done the will of God, you will receive what he has promised. For in just a very little while, "He who is coming will come and will not delay. But my righteous one will live by faith. And if he shrinks back, I will not be pleased with him." But we are not of those who shrink back and are destroyed, but of those who believe and are saved.

HEBREWS 10:35–39 NIV

In . . . silence we find a new energy and a real unity. God's energy becomes ours, allowing us to perform things well.

MOTHER TERESA

# Remember...

_____Trusting in God is the surest way to victory.

_____God's strength can become most apparent just when you feel your faith start to weaken.

_____When you place your faith in God and not in your religious activities, you take a big step toward uncomplicating your spiritual life.

_____God's second wind is more than enough to see you through to the finish line.

# Simplify...

Be persistent in your prayer request. Write it down, date it, and keep praying it as evidence of your faith that God will answer your prayer.

Focus on God and your relationship with him instead of the answer to your prayer.

Read the story of Joseph (Genesis 37—48) who faithfully waited for decades to see the promises of God come to fulfillment in his life.

Memorize Hebrews 10:35–39 and remember it when your faith sags.

Find a prayer partner, a trusted friend with whom you can share prayer concerns and mutual encouragement.

_With the Hebrews and the Greeks it was the national character and the spiritual creative energy of the people which endured._

HANS KOHN

# Do You Really Know What Time It Is?

Be very careful, then, how you live—not as unwise but as wise, making the most of every opportunity, because the days are evil.
Ephesians 5:15–16 NIV

Years ago, the lyricist of a popular rock song asked this question: Does anybody really know what time it is? Sure, you can look at your watch and the clock on the wall, but the only thing they tell you is the time according to a highly useful but man-made standard. When you begin to think in terms of eternity—the reality beyond the rotation of the planet—you realize that the way you spend your time on earth will have consequences in heaven. That long-range view helps keep you focused on the things that really matter and that helps simplify your list of priorities in life.

Look at all that Christ accomplished in three years of ministry on earth. To some, his was a promising life cut short by the tragic consequences of political and religious hostility. But viewed in terms of eternity, Jesus' short time on earth was all it took to complete his work. He made the most of his earthly life by being about his Father's business, a pattern he wants you and all believers to follow. When you follow his lead, you reduce the complications in your life caused by heading in the wrong direction altogether.

The Bible tells you to live carefully, making the most of every opportunity. Queen Esther, whose story is told in the biblical book of Esther, learned that lesson well. In the midst of an urgent situation—the almost certain destruction of her people—she took the time to carefully consider her actions and only then moved swiftly. God used her willingness to save the Jewish people. You may not be a member of a royal family, but your willingness to follow God's plan is no less important. By making the most of the opportunities he gives you, you can minister to others in ways that carry eternal significance.

As you learn to think in terms of the eternal consequences of your actions, your priorities begin to change. As serious as all that sounds, maintaining an eternal perspective on life can be exciting as you consider the great and glorious things God has in store for you to do.

## One Final Thought

Make the most of your time on earth by keeping an eternal perspective on all that you do.

# Thoughts for Simply Living

There is a time for everything, and a season for every
activity under heaven . . . a time to scatter stones
and a time to gather them . . . a time to be silent
and a time to speak.

ECCLESIASTES 3:1, 5, 7 NIV

Nothing valuable can be lost by taking time.

ABRAHAM LINCOLN

Whoever obeys [the King's] command will come
to no harm, and the wise heart will know the proper
time and procedure.

ECCLESIASTES 8:5 NIV

He who has no vision of eternity will never get a true hold of time.

THOMAS CARLYLE

# Remember...

_____Follow Jesus' example by always being about your heavenly Father's business.

_____Maintaining an eternal perspective keeps your time on earth in perspective.

_____What you do with your days on earth is more important than the number of your days on earth.

_____Obedience to God can result in an exciting life of ministry with eternal consequences.

## Simplify...

Read how Queen Esther made the most of an unusual opportunity and consider how following her example of timing could be applied to your life.

When you wake up each day, think first about how you will use your time in ways that will have an impact in eternity.

You are living in this day and age for a purpose; commit the rest of your life to fulfilling that purpose.

Begin to believe that God has great and glorious things in store for you to do.

Trust that God's schedule for bringing things to pass is far more accurate than your own timetable.

_Time is a child of eternity, and resembles its parent as much as it can._

DEAN W. R. INGE

# Your Toughest Competitor

Love each other deeply. Honor others more than yourselves.
Romans 12:10 NIrV

In the coming years, you will face competition on many fronts: at school, in sports, at work, even at church. Healthy competition—that which never turns degrading or demeaning—keeps you sharp and focused on the right things. Whenever you are focused on what God has called you to do, you simplify your life by eliminating pointless distractions, like paying too much attention to what the other guy is doing.

Likewise, any time you avoid unhealthy competition, you stand a better chance of maintaining your perspective on what is really important—and that includes your relationships with others. The Bible says that you should "'Love the Lord your God with all your heart and with all your soul and with all your strength and with all your mind'; and, 'Love your neighbor as yourself'" (Luke 10:27 NIV). And your best role model for the way you should treat unbelievers is Jesus himself, who reserved his contempt for the self-righteous Pharisees but treated the people around him with love and compassion. Whether the competition is with believers or unbelievers, you can treat them with love and compassion without losing your competitive edge.

It's easy to think of your biggest competition in terms of another person, but your toughest—and best—competitor is actually yourself. If you keep that in mind, you can avoid situations in which your competitive spirit could damage your relationships. By narrowing the field of competition to one person—yourself—you create a win-win environment. You win by making it your goal to be better in all that you do and all that you are, and by preserving your personal relationships in the process, thus simplifying your life. Others win by making your high standards their goal and learning from you how to compete in a respectful way.

You can quietly make your mark on the world by simply focusing on improving yourself. Your love for others must be of paramount importance whenever you find yourself in a competitive situation; your refusal to get involved in petty, mean-spirited competition will set you apart as a winner. Save your aggression for the challenges in life that really matter—like developing a godly character.

## One Final Thought

When you see yourself as your sole competitor, you help preserve your relationships with others.

# Thoughts for Simply Living

If anyone competes as an athlete, he does not receive the victor's crown unless he competes according to the rules.

2 TIMOTHY 2:5 NIV

The only person you should ever compete with is yourself.
You can't hope for a fairer match.

TODD ROTHMAN

Jesus said, "[I pray] that all of them may be one, Father, just as you are in me and I am in you. May they also be in us so that the world may believe that you have sent me."

JOHN 17:21 NIV

One of the most difficult lessons for ambitious young people to learn is that when you try to make an impression, that is the impression you make. Those whose center of emotional gravity is deeply embedded are willing to wait quietly in line until they are discovered.

SIDNEY HARRIS

# Remember...

_____Your personal relationships are important to God.

_____Competing against yourself creates a win-win situation for you and those around you.

_____Healthy competition is never demeaning or degrading to others.

When you learn to narrow the field of competition to yourself, you simplify your life.

# Simplify...

Ask God to help you compete only with yourself, not with those around you.

Lovingly pray for those who try to compete with you.

Read the quote by Sidney Harris and journal about how you can quietly become a winner.

Come up with at least one simple thing you can do to improve yourself.

Ask God to give you a deep desire for unity with other believers and compassion for unbelievers.

*With skills up our sleeve and God in our hearts, we just have to be winners.*

CECIL WILLIAMS

# Getting It Right the First Time

If you wander off the road to the right or the left, you will hear his voice behind you saying, "Here is the road. Follow it."

Isaiah 30:21 GNT

Have you ever tried to install a seemingly easy software program, only to discover that the installation wasn't as simple as you thought it would be? You probably have installed dozens of programs in the past without a hitch—and that may be the problem. You were so sure you knew what you were doing that you didn't read the instructions. The lesson for life is obvious: When you follow directions, you stand a much better chance for success in whatever you undertake.

The instructions for living life successfully are contained in the Bible, God's Word. You can't find a more reliable source than that. Do you genuinely want to live a simpler life? The book of Proverbs is like a treasure chest filled with valuable nuggets of wisdom that will help keep your life simple. The teachings of Jesus found throughout the Gospels and the direction given in the Epistles—basically, all the books between Acts and Revelation—also contain priceless information for living a life free of burdensome complications.

Your loving Father wants you to enjoy life as you serve him and other people, so he left you an incomparable book filled with guidelines for successful living. Far from being a complex, difficult-to-understand owner's manual, the Bible tells you how to live through the clarity and wisdom of its direct teaching and through the richness and power of the stories it records. What's more, God sent the Holy Spirit to reveal truth to you and give you ongoing, specific direction for the life God wants you to live.

God wants you to obey him not because he is a demanding, punishing God, but because he genuinely knows what is best for you. He made you for a purpose, and he wants you to fulfill that purpose. As you seek his direction and follow it, you may suddenly realize that you are living the kind of life you wanted to live all along, a simple life of faith in God.

## One Final Thought

When you follow God's directions for each step of your life, you can be assured of getting it right the first time.

# Thoughts for Simply Living

Your word is a lamp to guide me and a light for my path.

PSALMS 119:105 GNT

When you follow the Lord with burning love, it may happen that on the road of life you strike your foot against the stone of some passion and fall unexpectedly into sin; or else finding yourself in a muddy place, you may slip involuntarily and fall headlong. Each time you fail and in this way injure your body, you should get up again with the same eagerness as before, and continue to follow after your Lord until you reach him.

JOHN OF CARPATHOS

Many will give glory to God for your loyalty to the gospel of Christ.

2 CORINTHIANS 9:13 GNT

Obedience to God is the most infallible evidence of sincere and supreme love to him.

NATHANAEL EMMONS

# Remember...

_____God's Word contains all the instruction you need for living life successfully.

_____God's Spirit was sent to reveal truth to you and offer you specific direction.

_____You can always trust God to provide the right directions.

_____Instructions are useless unless you actually follow them.

# Simplify...

Get to know what the Bible says about the way you should live. Jesus' teachings in the Gospels are a great place to start.

Meditate on the Ten Commandments and the ways in which obeying them can simplify your life.

Learn to identify God's voice by comparing what you believe he has said to you with what the Bible says; he will never give you direction that is contrary to Scripture.

Memorize Psalm 119:105.

When you are not sure what to do, look for answers in God's Word and memorize them so you will know what to do in any situation.

*Most of us would rather risk catastrophe than read a direction.*

MIGNON MCLAUGHLIN

# Lessons from an Ant

He who gathers money little by little makes it grow.
Proverbs 13:11 NIV

Did you ever have an ant farm? Lots of kids have spent hours in amusement as they watched the ants work away between the sand-filled panes of glass. In fact, ants are so industrious—and fascinating to watch—that they are used as an example in the Bible.

Proverbs 6 suggests that by observing the ways of ants, you can discover financial wisdom. That's because the work of ants reaps not only immediate benefits but also long-term gains; the ants store up provisions for later, even while meeting their present needs. In doing so, the ants avoid the complications caused by lack of resources later on.

The financial lesson is obvious. If you set aside money as you work, your savings will be there in an emergency or when you are no longer able to work. God considers this to be good stewardship, or taking good care of what he has given you. By providing for your future, you won't have to tap into resources intended for others in need, and you won't have to complicate your life by scrambling for extra income.

But remember that hoarding is not the same as saving. Hoarding is based on greed—you want more and more stored up for yourself, so you keep more than you need. Meanwhile, people throughout the world, even in your own town, are dying from the effects of poverty, and worthwhile charities and missions continue to be seriously underfunded. Saving money to care for yourself and your future family is right and responsible in the eyes of God; hoarding money in a greedy quest for more and better is never acceptable in God's sight.

Start saving now, even if you can only set aside a few dollars a week. Not only will you be contributing to your own future, you will also be learning to live on less than you make—a valuable and important step toward a lifestyle of simplicity, and one that you will never regret. No matter how meager your current contribution, keep in mind that the Bible says the person who "gathers money little by little makes it grow." Saving is good, but your reliance should always be on God, not on your own efforts to increase your savings.

## One Final Thought

No matter how much money you save, you need to place your security and confidence in God alone.

# Thoughts for Simply Living

The best food and olive oil are stored up in the houses of
wise people. But a foolish man eats up everything he has.

PROVERBS 21:20 NIrV

Make all you can, save all you can, give all you can.

JOHN WESLEY

Go to the ant, you sluggard; consider its ways and be wise!
It has no commander, no overseer or ruler, yet it stores
its provisions in summer and gathers its food at harvest.

PROVERBS 6:6–8 NIV

Buying, possessing, accumulating—this is not worldliness. But doing this in
the love of it, with no love of God paramount—doing it so that thoughts
of eternity and God are an intrusion—doing it so that one's spirit is
secularized in the process; this is worldliness.

HERRICK JOHNSON

# Remember...

_____You can start helping your future spouse and children by saving for the future now.

_____When you learn to live on less than you earn, you help keep your life free of financial debt and worry.

_____Stewardship includes taking good care of your future as well as your present.

_____You can rely on God to show you how to manage your finances so you can save and give and still have enough to live on.

# Simplify...

Start saving immediately, no matter how little you have to start with.

Learn about different savings plans. Ask God to show you which is best for you.

Draw up a personal budget and include a percentage of your income to save.

Keep contributing to your savings account, but learn to ignore the balance; let it accumulate without obsessing over it.

Ask God to keep you from placing your security and confidence in anything—or anyone—but him.

*Saving is greater than earning.*

GERMAN PROVERB

# Simple Living
## Possessions

Jesus said, "Watch out and guard yourselves from every kind of greed; because your true life is not made up of the things you own, no matter how rich you may be."
LUKE 12:15 GNT

Dependence upon material possessions inevitably results in the destruction of human character.

AGNES E. MEYER

We brought nothing into the world, and we can take nothing out of it. But if we have food and clothing, we will be content with that. People who want to get rich fall into temptation and a trap.
1 TIMOTHY 6:7–9 NIV

I have learned to be satisfied with what I have. I know what it is to be in need and what it is to have more than enough. I have learned this secret, so that anywhere, at any time, I am content, whether I am full or hungry, whether I have too much or too little. I have the strength to face all conditions by the power that Christ gives me.
PHILIPPIANS 4:11–13 GNT

He owns the cattle on a thousand hills,
The wealth in every mine;
He owns the rivers and the rocks and rills,
The sun and stars that shine.

Wonderful riches, more than tongue can tell—
He is my Father so they're mine as well;
He owns the cattle on a thousand hills—
I know that He will care for me.

JOHN W. PETERSON

# Brain Clutter

Trust in God at all times, O people; pour out your hearts to him,
for God is our refuge.
Psalm 62:8 NIV

Do you know where a great amount of clutter in your
life tends to accumulate? In your brain. Think of all that you
have to consciously remember on a single weekday: school
assignments, locker combination, after-school activities,
family responsibilities, and much more. Meanwhile, your
subconscious is constantly at work as thoughts come and go
throughout the day. After a while, your brain can become
like an overloaded computer whose files are in disarray. In
computer jargon that means you need to run the disk
defragmenter; in real life, it means you need to sort out your
thoughts. A good way to make sense out of brain clutter is
to write in a journal about what's on your mind.

People who keep a journal on a regular basis often say
that their private writing has helped them simplify the
problems in their lives. Writing down your thoughts helps
you to think more clearly. As you write, your ideas begin to
take shape—physically in the words your hand forms and

physiologically in the structure your brain creates. Seeing the words on paper helps your brain store the information in a more organized way, and that helps you to see your problems more clearly.

When you make entries in your journal you are writing for you—and God—alone. Don't worry about how your writing sounds; be concerned only that it's honest and open. If you've become accustomed to writing on a computer, you may have to relearn how to write with your hand. You can keep a journal on your hard drive, but it may not be as helpful as one that you write out longhand. This is so because writing with your hand slows you down which may prompt you to give serious thought to the words you are using—the point to journaling in the first place.

Journaling is a useful tool to help clarify your thoughts and focus on difficult concepts, facts, and questions. Best of all, journaling can be a form of prayer as you share your thoughts with God through your writing and sort out the difficulties in your personal life.

## One Final Thought

Keep your thoughts straight by picking up a pen and writing about what's on your mind—for only you and God to see.

# Thoughts for Simply Living

[Luke wrote] Many have undertaken to draw up an account of the things that have been fulfilled among us . . . Therefore, since I myself have carefully investigated everything from the beginning, it seemed good also to me to write an orderly account for you.

LUKE 1:1, 3 NIV

We do not write in order to be understood; we write in order to understand.

CECIL DAY LEWIS

[Paul wrote] We do not write you anything you cannot read or understand. And I hope that, as you have understood us in part, you will come to understand fully.

2 CORINTHIANS 1:13–14 NIV

Writing crystallizes thought, and thought produces action.

PAUL J. MEYER

# Remember...

_____Writing from your heart, for you and God alone, will help to clarify your thinking.

_____Striving to write accurately and honestly will help to streamline your thinking.

_____Writing will help you share your thoughts with God.

_____God told his people to write down his words so they would not forget his commands or his goodness to them.

# Simplify...

Keep a notebook next to your bed; write down thoughts that come to you if you wake up during the night.

Begin keeping a journal as regularly as is practical for you.

Copy a psalm or chapter of the Bible into your journal; see what new insights you acquire for simplifying your life.

Use your journal to get rid of brain clutter.

Reach for your notebook in the early morning and start writing whatever comes to mind before you're fully awake. Your words may pleasantly surprise you later on.

*Crossroad moments of life may merit several journal entries.*

Susan Annette Muto

81

# Fully Aware, Fully Alive

God is able to make all grace abound to you, so that in all things at all times, having all that you need, you will abound in every good work.

2 Corinthians 9:8 NIV

Intentional living means being fully aware of your surroundings, paying careful attention to everything said and done in your presence, and being open to what God might be asking you to do in a given situation. It's a way of living that many people are learning to follow, especially people with a deep and active faith in God who yearn for a simpler life.

You probably feel as if most of your days fly by in a flurry of activity. Everything in your life is so fast-paced that it may seem impossible to be aware of so many details. God, however, gave you life to enjoy. He wants you to be completely present in all things at all times by paying attention to what is happening and being said—rather than to what you anticipate happening and being said—and being available to him for service. Jesus and the New Testament writers frequently encouraged believers to be alert. In 1 Thessalonians 5:6, Paul particularly urged

Christians to avoid going through life in a kind of fog.

When you go through your day thoughtful of God's presence in your life, your mind and body automatically slow down. You find yourself looking and listening more carefully when another person is talking to you. Your spirit becomes more sensitive to God's leading, because you are more spiritually aware. Focusing on God and others keeps you from being distracted by unimportant things, and your life becomes simpler.

The story of the Good Samaritan is about compassion that also serves as an example of intentional living. Unlike the priest and the Levite, the Samaritan saw beyond inconvenience to himself and did what was necessary to help a fellow human being in need. God wants that kind of awareness from all of his people.

Make a conscious effort to be more aware in your encounters with others. Attend to what is going on at the moment. Focus on being open to God's intentions and finding purpose in your interactions.

## One Final Thought

When you are aware of God's presence, you can offer more of him to others.

# Thoughts for Simply Living

Teach us to number our days aright, that we may gain a
heart of wisdom.

PSALM 90:12 NIV

I don't want to get to the end of my life and find that I lived just the length of it.
I want to live the width of it as well.

DIANE ACKERMAN

A Samaritan, as he traveled, came where the man who had
been beaten and robbed was; and when he saw him, he took
pity on him. He went to him and bandaged his wounds,
pouring on oil and wine. Then he put the man on his own
donkey, took him to an inn and took care of him. The next
day he took out two silver coins and gave them to the
innkeeper. "Look after him," he said, "and when I return, I
will reimburse you for any extra expense you may have."

LUKE 10:33–35 NIV

A man is ethical only when life, as such, is sacred to him, that of plants and
animals as that of his fellow men, and when he devotes himself helpfully
to all life that is in need of help.

ALBERT SCHWEITZER

# Remember...

_____Being fully present means being consciously aware of what is going on at the moment.

_____Intentional living makes you more sensitive to God's leading and activity in your life.

_____When you live intentionally, you automatically slow down and become more receptive to God speaking to you.

_____You show regard for others when you give them your full attention.

# Simplify...

Practice intentional living as you go through your day tomorrow.

> Make notes on how intentional living changes the pace of your day from hectic to calm.

Do some brainstorming and come up with different ways that the daily practice of intentional living could simplify your life.

> Read the story of the Good Samaritan found in Luke 10 and consider how it relates to intentional living.

Practice intentional living in your dealings with others.

*Your purpose is the essence of who you are. It is the reason you are alive.*

IDELETTE VAN PAPENDORP

# Looking Back

I will remember the deeds of the LORD; yes, I will remember
your miracles of long ago.
Psalm 77:11 NIV

You've grown up in a world of rapidly changing
technology. You've come to anticipate significant changes in
communications, computers, and the entertainment media.
You look to see what's ahead before you invest in a gadget
that will be obsolete in a few months, and you realize that
technology has become so complex that even buying it is
now complicated. There's always something more advanced
on the horizon.

All that forward thinking threatens to make the past
seem, well, passé, and not just in the field of technology. In
so many aspects of contemporary life, people believe that if
something is not new, it is not relevant. But that's hardly a
twenty-first-century phenomenon, because thousands of
years ago God had to remind the Israelites that they needed
to remember the past—the history they had as a nation and
the history of their relationship with him. He knew they
would strengthen their faith by remembering past events—

particularly the many times God performed miracles on their behalf and spared them from destruction. What's more, if they applied the lessons they learned to their present situation, they could avoid a great deal of sin, misery, and heartache.

When you understand all that God has done for you and for people throughout history, you are better equipped to recognize his activity in your life and in society right now. You will know you can trust him, because you know how he has come through for you and for other people in the past. When you apply the lessons he has taught you in the past to your present circumstances, you avoid making the same mistakes all over again, and that leads to a simpler life.

You can still look forward to the future. Just remember also to look back at what God has done for you. Look at what he did for the Israelites in the Old Testament and the early church in the New Testament. Learn from what you read and what you have experienced with God, and allow your faith to gain strength as a result.

## One Final Thought

By looking at what went before, you can better
understand what is and what will be.

# Thoughts for Simply Living

Remember the days of old. Think about what the LORD did through those many years. Ask your father. He will tell you. Ask your elders. They'll explain it to you.

DEUTERONOMY 32:7 NIrV

All history is incomprehensible without Christ.

ERNEST RENAN

Give thanks to the LORD, call on his name; make known among the nations what he has done. Sing to him, sing praise to him; tell of all his wonderful acts. Glory in his holy name; let the hearts of those who seek the LORD rejoice. Look to the LORD and his strength; seek his face always. Remember the wonders he has done, his miracles, and the judgments he pronounced.

PSALM 105:1–5 NIV

The best way to suppose what may come is to remember what is past.

GEORGE SAVILE

# Remember...

_____When you learn from the past, you can avoid mistakes now and in the future.

_____You can better interpret current events when you have a good handle on God's activity in history.

_____You strengthen your faith as you recall how God has worked in the past.

_____What people have learned throughout history can be just as relevant for you today as it was for them.

# Simplify...

List in your journal details of some of the lessons God taught you in the past.

Apply the principles you just listed to a present situation

Resolve not to have to repeat one of those lessons, and plan how you'll accomplish this.

Read Hebrews 11 to see how God worked through people of faith in the past.

The writer of Ecclesiastes believed "there is nothing new under the sun" (Ecclesiastes 1:9 NIV). Meditate on that thought.

_There is no humorist like history._

WILL AND ARIEL DURANT

# Free to Love

Jesus said, "Love your enemies and pray for those who persecute you."
Matthew 5:43–44 NRSV

Being asked to forgive someone, even when you feel that the other person's actions are pretty close to being unforgivable, is a challenge. If you have been asked to forgive someone and managed to do so, however, you've discovered a wonderful secret: you know how much better you felt afterward. After you let go of the grudge, life got easier. It's not easy to forgive others, but it's worth it. When you release your resentment through the act of forgiveness, you demolish the barriers that threaten to destroy your relationships and complicate your life.

Jesus frequently spoke to his followers about the attitude he wanted them to have toward people who persecuted them, maligned them, or just plain irritated them. You've read his sayings: "Love your enemies," "Turn the other cheek," "Forgive others as you have been forgiven." Some believers think it isn't fair that Christians should make so many concessions. But those who think this fail to see what Jesus knew so well, that those who forgive receive a double blessing: a restored relationship and the freedom to move on. Resentment keeps you stuck in a rut as you keep replaying the offending incident in your head. Forgiveness clears your thoughts and your heart and releases you from the complex schemes of a vengeful mind.

You've probably heard about people who have borne a lifelong grudge against others and realized too late that they wasted their lives on resentment. You've probably also heard people say something like, "I could never forgive her for that!" Don't be like them. Don't set yourself up for a lifetime of misery. Get rid of resentment the moment it appears and keep your relationships free of the nagging complications caused by unforgiven wrongs.

Are you harboring a grudge that has hindered your ability to love someone? If so, forgive the person immediately. Maybe the offense is one that only you are aware of. Forgive the person anyway in the privacy of your own heart. Lay down the grudge and never pick it up again. Be free of it. It may not be easy, but it will certainly simplify your life.

## One Final Thought

Keep your mind and heart free to love others by
keeping yourself free of resentment.

# *Thoughts for Simply Living*

Jesus said, "If you forgive others the wrongs they have done to you, your Father in heaven will also forgive you."
MATTHEW 6:14 GNT

To carry a grudge is like being stung to death by one bee.
WILLIAM H. WALTON

Paul wrote: Get rid of all bitterness, rage and anger, brawling and slander, along with every form of malice.
EPHESIANS 4:31 NIV

Resentment toward any human being cannot exist in the same heart with love to God.
WILLIAM T. HAM

# Remember...

_____Forgiveness allows you to move on with your life.

_____Forgiveness restores your relationships with God and other people.

_____With forgiveness comes freedom.

_____A loving attitude toward your enemies pleases God and makes your life easier.

## Simplify...

Consciously forgive anyone you have been holding a grudge against.

Confess your resentment to God and accept his forgiveness.

Let go of your resentment in favor of freedom.

Deliberately fill your heart with God.

Pray for those you consider your enemies.

*Doing an injury puts you below your enemy;*
*revenging one makes you but even with him;*
*forgiving it sets you above him.*

AUTHOR UNKNOWN

# The Care of Your Spirit

Physical training is of some value, but godliness has value for all things, holding promise for both the present life and the life to come.

1 Timothy 4:8 NIV

You've had health classes throughout your years in school. You've learned a great deal about nutrition, exercise, and hygiene. You are perhaps beginning to realize that by developing health-related habits now, you may ward off complex health problems later on. But did you know that you can develop healthy habits in your spiritual life?

Throughout the Bible images of food are used to describe the need for spiritual nourishment: bread in Matthew 4:4 and elsewhere in the Gospels, milk in 1 Peter 2:2, and both milk and meat in Hebrews 5:12–14, just to name a few. Exercise is evident in biblical references that compare the faith journey to training for a race, and even today people speak of exercising their faith and doing spiritual exercises, such as prayer, Bible reading, and meditation. When it comes to spiritual hygiene, images of purity and cleanliness abound in the Bible.

What this means for you is that you can train yourself to

begin to think in terms of spiritual health. Do you hear your stomach growl during second period? Let it remind you of the need for spiritual food as well—taking in the spiritual nutrients of the word of God and digesting it. Allow physical education and sports activities to remind you of the need to exercise your faith by stepping out and trusting God for something. As you shower or brush your teeth, think of how the power of God has cleansed you from impure thoughts, motives, and actions.

You can have a healthy spiritual life by developing a few spiritual routines that you practice daily. They don't have to be complicated or time-consuming; you want to simplify your life, not pile on additional obligations! Simple routines help structure your day. Brushing your teeth is a good example. A simple routine can make a huge difference in your day. In a similar way, an activity such as prayer—simple, unadorned conversation with God—can become such an important part of your routine that you wouldn't think of leaving the house in the morning or falling asleep at night without talking and listening to God first.

## One Final Thought

When your spirit is healthy, you are better able to serve God and others.

# Thoughts for Simply Living

Find out for yourself how good the LORD is. Happy are those who find safety with him. Honor the LORD, all his people; those who obey him have all they need. Even lions go hungry for lack of food, but those who obey the LORD lack nothing good.

PSALM 34:8–10 GNT

We are truly indefatigable in providing for the needs of the body, but we starve the soul.

ELLEN WOOD

Jesus said, "It is written: 'Man does not live on bread alone, but on every word that comes from the mouth of God.'"

MATTHEW 4:4 NIV

You no more need a day off from spiritual concentration in matters of life than your heart needs a day off from beating. As you cannot take a day off morally and remain moral, you cannot take a day off spiritually and remain spiritual.

OSWALD CHAMBERS

# Remember...

_____Your spirit needs to be taken care of as much as your body does.

_____The word of God is the most nutritious bread you can feed your spirit.

_____Exercising your faith keeps you spiritually fit.

_____A healthy spirit is one that is free of moral impurity.

# Simplify...

Quietly sit in God's presence for a few minutes at the beginning of each day to help structure your day.

Ask God to show you what you need to do to get spiritually fit.

Make a list of practices that are unhealthy for you spiritually and resolve to rid yourself of them.

Form the habit of consciously thanking God for the good that happens to you.

List those things you experience that could serve as reminders of the need for spiritual health (such as your growling stomach reminding you to feed your spirit).

_Watch out for a "spiritual stuttering" that puts an endless series of obstructions between us and our spiritual goal._

SAM KEEN

# Simple Living
## Responsibilities

Sweetest Lord, make me appreciative of the dignity of my high vocation, and its many responsibilities. Never permit me to disgrace it by giving way to coldness, unkindness, or impatience.

MOTHER TERESA

*"Well done, you good and faithful servant!" said his master. "You have been faithful in managing small amounts, so I will put you in charge of large amounts. Come on in and share my happiness!"*
MATTHEW 25:21 GNT

*Never tire of doing what is right.*
2 THESSALONIANS 3:13 NIV

*Only someone with no sense would promise to be responsible for someone else's debts.*
PROVERBS 17:18 GNT

Rejoice in your responsibilities.
Fulfill them gladly,
That you might be fulfilled.

There is no shorter path
To a difficult life
Than responsibilities neglected.

There is no shorter path
To maturity
Than responsibilities embraced.

TIMOTHY FILSTON

# Recharge, Refresh, Refocus

For God alone my soul waits in silence.
Psalm 62:5 NRSV

Have you ever "heard" complete silence? Few people have, and those who have often say they find the absence of sound to be disturbing. Sound reminds you that you live in an active environment filled with living beings and functioning machines whose noise frequently vies for your attention. When your environment gets to be too much, though, you need to leave the jangled sounds behind and seek quiet so that you can hear yourself think. By reducing the amount of noises around you, you can better zero in on your own thoughts.

Jesus himself frequently distanced himself from noise. Throughout the Gospels, you see him retreating from the ever-present crowds and spending quiet time with a few friends or with God the Father alone. Quiet times served to recharge his energy, refresh his spirit, and refocus his attention on the purpose for which God sent him. That's a pretty good pattern to follow. Recharge, refresh, refocus—

imagine how the complex jumble of daily life would sort itself out if you could take advantage of those three transforming activities once in a while.

If you live in a thin-walled apartment building or on a traffic-snarled city street, it may be a challenge to get away from the constant noise. Try masking outside noises by using headphones to listen to relaxing instrumental music. You can also try white noise, available in various brands of sound machines. White noise is an unobtrusive sound that serves to block out or mask unwanted environmental noise.

You won't always be able to control the sounds around you, but exercise what control you have—keep the volume down, retreat from raucous crowds, speak quietly. Use your quiet time to meditate, refocus, and pray. Keep it simple. You'll discover that your thinking will become clearer and your nerves calmer.

## One Final Thought

When you give your mind a rest from the din of everyday life, you settle into a calmer, less frenetic state of mind.

# Thoughts for Simply Living

In repentance and rest is your salvation, in quietness and trust is your strength.

ISAIAH 30:15 NIV

Silence is more musical than any song.

CHRISTINA ROSSETTI

The fruit of righteousness will be peace; the effect of righteousness will be quietness and confidence forever.

ISAIAH 32:17 NIV

True silence is the rest of the mind. It is to the spirit what sleep is to the body—nourishment and refreshment.

WILLIAM PENN

# Remember...

_____Reducing the noise in your life helps you think more clearly.

_____Like Jesus, you need to spend quiet time with God.

_____Even if you can't find a quiet place, you can probably find a way to eliminate some of the noise in your environment.

_____Reflection, prayer, and meditation come easier when you turn down the noise around you.

# Simplify...

Take a walk through the woods or a park or another quiet place. Pray silently as you walk and be attentive to any thoughts you feel are from God.

Sit in the presence of God in the quietest place you can find. Simply enjoy being in his presence.

Try masking the noise around you with soft instrumental music or a tape of nature sounds like ocean waves.

Lower the volume on the stereo or television a notch or two and get used to that setting.

Block out any noise and create a quite time every day simply to relax and recharge.

*I never miss a good chance to shut up.*

JAMES PATTERSON

# The "You" You Were Meant to Be

I praise you because I am fearfully and wonderfully made;
your works are wonderful, I know that full well.

Psalm 139:14 NIV

If someone were to ask, "Who are you, really?" you'd probably suspect he was looking for a more substantial answer than your name. A list of labels might come to mind: Christian, sophomore, sibling, friend, math wizard, and so on. But this someone wants to know more, like who you are deep down inside, what makes you tick, what sets you off, what brings you joy or despair. Without a true understanding of that level of yourself, you may not know just who you are. Make it your goal to know who God intended you to be, which makes life a great deal easier than trying to be someone you're not.

God created each person as a distinct individual. No one in history has ever been and no one in the future will ever be exactly like you (even if cloning becomes successful, because no lab can clone your spirit—your most distinctive aspect). Psalm 139 underscores the idea of individual uniqueness. In verse 13 David wrote to the Lord, "You created my inmost being." God created your "inmost being"—your soul, your spirit, the real you—and he is the one who can reveal its deepest secrets and treasures to you.

Getting to know the "you" you were meant to be can eliminate a host of potential complications. Think back to your earliest memories: What piqued your interest? What have you most enjoyed doing? What gives you a sense of satisfaction? Consider this: the better you know yourself, the easier it will be to make better dating decisions. You'll be able to tell immediately when someone is wrong for you, no matter how appealing he or she may be. The same principle applies to other decisions, like which college to attend. If you realize that big cities make you edgy, for example, you know you should limit your search to schools in rural or suburban areas.

What matters most is to know who you are in relation to God—to know that you are his child and that he knows everything about your "inmost being" and is willing to share that information with you. You can't discover that kind of knowledge about yourself in any other way.

## One Final Thought

As you get to know yourself better, you cannot help but stand in awe of God and the love he has for his human creation.

# Thoughts for Simply Living

[O LORD,] your hands made me and formed me;
give me understanding to learn your commands.

PSALM 119:73 NIV

Let me know myself, Lord, and I shall know thee.

SAINT AUGUSTINE OF HIPPO

God's whole nature is living in Christ in human form.
Because you belong to Christ, you have everything you
need. He is the ruler over every power and authority.
When you received Christ, you were also circumcised
by putting away your sinful nature. Human hands
didn't circumcise you. Christ did. When you were
baptized, you were buried together with him. You were
raised to life together with him by believing in God's
power. God raised Jesus from the dead.

COLOSSIANS 2:9–12 NIrV

What can we gain by sailing to the moon if we are not able to cross the abyss
that separates us from ourselves? This is the most important of all voyages of
discovery, and without it, all the rest are not only useless, but disastrous.

THOMAS MERTON

# Remember...

_____Getting to know yourself helps you appreciate the care that God took in making you.

_____God can reveal to you the secrets of your "inmost being."

_____Who you are in relation to God is the most important aspect of who you are.

_____Knowing yourself better has practical as well as spiritual benefits.

# Simplify...

Thank God for making you the way you are.

Ask God to show you the real you—the you he intends for you to be. Wait quietly for his answer.

Meditate on Psalm 139 and try memorizing it.

Make a list of the practical ways in which knowing yourself better could improve your life (such as the dating example).

As you discover new things about yourself, be sure to enter your thoughts in your journal.

_No amount of self-improvement can make up for
a lack of self-acceptance._

ROBERT HOLDEN

# The Mind of Christ

Wisdom is supreme; therefore get wisdom. Though it cost all you have, get understanding.
Proverbs 4:7 NIV

You work hard to get good grades. You know that your grades have to meet a certain standard if you plan to attend college, if you want to show your parents that you're giving school your best shot, or if your goal is simply to graduate. At times, though, you may wonder, "When am I ever going to use this stuff? I'm planning to teach English—why do I need algebra?" Well, understanding a few biblical principles would help simplify your life in school and transform the way you think about education.

God made you to be a productive human being. Right now, he has given you a job to do, and that job is going to school and acquiring knowledge. But there's much more involved than cramming your head full of facts and information. As a believer, you have the mind of Christ. That means that Christ willingly imparts his wisdom to you, helping you to apply the principles behind the knowledge you acquire to the way you live.

An incident in history, when seen through a biblical lens, can help you better understand a current crisis in the world and how you should respond to it as a Christian. Applying the wisdom of Christ to literature can give you an extraordinary understanding of human nature. And algebra? Its benefits are many. Perhaps for you it might be a way to learn or how to puzzle out a complex problem.

Grades are important, but far more important is having a good grasp on how the things you learn apply to your life—and a good grasp on the process of learning itself. Success in those two areas will help make you a lifelong learner, a person who continues to acquire knowledge even when no one is handing out grades anymore. Add to that the wisdom Christ imparts to you, and you have a recipe for success in life. In the meantime, you can save yourself academic frustration by keeping your focus on the purpose of knowledge for you as a believer.

## One Final Thought

When you look beyond your grades to the wisdom God wants to give you, your goals as a student automatically become easier to achieve.

# Thoughts for Simply Living

**The fear of the Lord is the beginning of knowledge.**
PROVERBS 1:7 NIV

They know enough who know how to learn.
HENRY ADAMS

The LORD gives wisdom, and from his mouth come
knowledge and understanding . . . you will understand what
is right and just and fair—every good path. For wisdom will
enter your heart, and knowledge will be pleasant to your
soul. Discretion will protect you, and understanding will
guard you.
PROVERBS 2:6, 9–11 NIV

The best-educated human being is the one who understands most about the
life in which he is placed.
HELEN KELLER

# Remember...

_____You have the greatest academic advantage ever—the mind of Christ.

_____God's wisdom makes knowledge more than simply a collection of facts and information.

_____The wisdom you acquire can help you better understand events and human nature from God's perspective.

_____When you focus on the true purpose of education, your academic goals become clearer

# Simplify...

Ask God to give you his wisdom as you do your schoolwork.

> Using an online Bible search, find out what the book of Proverbs has to say about wisdom.

Spend a few minutes simply thinking about what it means to have the mind of Christ.

> The next time you have a graded homework assignment, concentrate as much on learning as on the grade you hope to get.

Memorize Proverbs 4:7.

*It is easier to educate a man when he wants to learn.*

NELSON MANDELA

# Watch Out for Worthless Things

"Think carefully about what you hear," Jesus said.
Mark 4:24 NIrV

Quick—without passing judgment on yourself—how much time each day do you estimate you spend on the phone? What do you talk about? Can you estimate the time you spend watching TV or videos? What kind of shows or movies do you generally watch? Maybe you feel you handle your time on the phone or in front of the TV responsibly. Even so, if you are like most Americans, both young and old, you probably spend a fair amount of time in those pursuits. While there's nothing inherently wrong with either one, both have the potential to complicate your life in a number of ways.

There is, of course, the issue of time. People often spend so much time in idle conversation on the phone or in watching pointless TV that they often end up scrambling around to get things done so they can start the whole process over again the following day. Time is not the only issue, however. At least as important for you as a believer is what you talk about on the phone and what you watch on television.

Proverbs 10:19 says that "When words are many, sin is not absent, but he who holds his tongue is wise." Long, rambling phone conversations provide the perfect medium for sin to flourish in. It's all too easy to stray into negative areas like spreading gossip and betraying confidences. With relevance for TV and videos, the Bible frequently admonishes God's people to keep their eyes from "worthless things" (Psalm 119:37). No one has to tell you how many "worthless things" you can watch in the space of just one hour.

Any time you do things that are pleasing to God, you remove the complication of potential sin from your life. Keep your mouth and ears free from the potential sin that long conversations on the telephone can lead you into. Keep your eyes and ears pure by radically restricting the type and amount of television you watch. Remember that your time and your right relationship with God are much too important to waste. Give careful attention to both.

## One Final Thought

Weigh the worth of the activities you pursue, and watch out for worthless investments of your time and interest.

# Thoughts for Simply Living

I will sing of your love and justice; to you, O LORD, I will sing praise . . . I will set before my eyes no vile thing. The deeds of faithless men I hate; they will not cling to me. Men of perverse heart shall be far from me; I will have nothing to do with evil.

PSALM 101:1, 3–4 NIV

Television was not intended to make human beings vacuous.

MALCOLM MUGGERIDGE

The psalmist wrote: Turn my eyes away from worthless things; preserve my life according to your word.

PSALM 119:37 NIV

[Television] has spread the habit of instant reaction and stimulated the hope of instant results.

ARTHUR M. SCHLESINGER JR.

# Remember...

_____What you see and hear has direct bearing on how you live your life.

_____Time is precious. Doing nothing—relaxing, that is—is more productive than wasting time on something worthless.

_____God wants you to keep yourself pure—and that includes your eyes and ears.

_____A right relationship with God depends in part on your willingness to take his admonitions seriously.

## Simplify...

Turn off the television for at least a week and use the time to write in your journal about the difference this makes in your life.

Monitor your telephone time, and make each call count.

Ask God to help you spend less time on worthless activities.

Come up with a schedule and a set of standards for watching TV and videos. Ask your parents for input.

Read Psalm 10:1–4 and consider whether you save room for God in your thoughts.

_Cinema, radio, television, magazines are a school of inattention: people look without seeing, listen in without hearing._

ROBERT BRESSON

# Free from the Web

Here is what people who belong to this world do. They try to satisfy what their sinful natures want to do. They long for what their sinful eyes look at. They brag about what they have and what they do. All of this comes from the world. It doesn't come from the Father

1 John 2:16 NIrV

Do you dream in HTML? Do you stare at the computer screen in disbelief when your e-mail program declares, "No new messages"? Do you think "@" is the middle name of your friends? If those questions sound familiar, you've probably read them—where else?—on the Internet. Numerous sites poke fun at people who spend too much time on the Internet. You may have seen some of the humorous tests and top-ten lists. But spending too much time on the Internet is no laughing matter. It can have serious and disturbing consequences in your life. The medium that helps simplify the lives of many who use it can complicate the lives of those who abuse it.

You can readily see how dependence on this medium runs counter to the way God wants you to live. The problem is not the Internet itself; the problem is the potential for online activity to become a substitute for life itself—and for God. Even if you restrict your Internet use to wholesome sites, you can deceive yourself into thinking that the people you know through online Bible studies and Christian chat rooms are really your friends or that the time you spend surfing Christian Web sites is time spent with God. Both are deceptions. The anonymity you and others have on the Internet creates even greater opportunities for deception.

If you believe this may be a problem for you, seek help. Turn to God first in repentance, asking him to forgive you for placing the Internet above him and the very real relationships you have in your very real life. Then seek help elsewhere, from a pastor or other trusted adult. Of course, there's plenty of help on the Internet, but you might want to have your counselor check out those resources. Or you may want to stay away from online activity altogether until your priorities are in order.

Have confidence that when you moderate your Internet activities, you'll experience freedom from "needing" to surf the Net.

## One Final Thought

God has promised you a life of freedom. That's the truth—and it's the truth that sets you free.

# Thoughts for Simply Living

Jesus said, "You will know the truth, and the truth will set you free."

JOHN 8:32 NIV

The Internet is so big, so powerful, and pointless that for some people it is a complete substitute for life.

ANDREW BROWN

Let the Lord make you strong. Depend on his mighty power. Put on all of God's armor. Then you can stand firm against the devil's evil plans. Our fight is not against human beings. It is against the rulers, the authorities and powers of this dark world. It is against the spiritual forces of evil in the heavenly world. So put on all of God's armor. Evil days will come. But you will be able to stand up to anything. And after you have done everything you can, you will still be standing.

EPHESIANS 6:10–13 NIrV

Every form of addiction is bad.

CARL JUNG

# Remember...

_____God is bigger than the Internet. He has the power to help you overcome anything.

_____God wants you to live a fulfilling life in your immediate environment and to interact with others in person.

_____Christ set you free—trust him to keep you free.

_____Know that your decisions affect your life—so avoid basing your decisions on what other people may do.

## Simplify...

If you think you may be spending too much time on the Internet, take the test at <www.netaddiction.com>.

Get professional Christian help if you believe you have a problem.

Estimate the amount of time you spend per week on the Internet and journal about how your life would be simpler without such a time-consuming distraction.

Ask God to break the hold the Internet has on you.

Enlist the help of a family member or close friend to hold you accountable as you try to break free of your addiction.

_Break a bad habit—drop it._

AUTHOR UNKNOWN

# Simple Living
## Money

Our Father holds the purse-strings, and . . . we may rest assured that he will provide for us. The Lord will be no man's debtor at the last. Saints know that a grain of heart's-ease is of more value than a ton of gold.

CHARLES H. SPURGEON

Jesus said, "No one can serve two masters. Either he will hate the one and love the other, or he will be devoted to the one and despise the other. You cannot serve both God and Money."

MATTHEW 6:24 NIV

Jesus said, "It is easier for a camel to go through the eye of a needle than for a rich man to enter the Kingdom of God."

MATTHEW 19:24 NIV

What good is it for a man to gain the whole world, yet forfeit his soul?

MARK 8:36 NIV

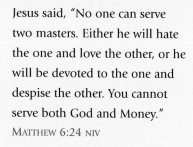

Money can buy a house, but not a home.

It can buy medicine, but not health.

It can buy a bed, but not sleep.

It can buy food, but not appetite.

It can buy finery, but not beauty.

It can buy a clock, but not time.

It can buy a book, but not knowledge.

It can buy a position, but not respect.

It can buy insurance, but not safety.

It can buy amusement, but not happiness.

AUTHOR UNKNOWN

# Contagious Actions

As God's chosen people, holy and dearly loved, clothe yourselves with compassion, kindness, humility, gentleness and patience.

Colossians 3:12 NIV

Think about the ways people have been kind to you recently. Those acts of kindness really stand out in your memory, don't they? One reason is that genuine acts of kindness—those that carry no conditions or expectation of return—are so rare, and yet these simple acts make life so much better. Wouldn't you like to spread that sort of kindness around? There's nothing complicated about it. You can perform both little and big acts of kindness day in and day out by developing a heart of compassion and a sensitivity to the opportunities for kindness that God provides for you. Focusing on others frees you from worrying about yourself and helps you to use time more productively.

You can't read the Bible, especially the New Testament, for very long without coming across a story, passage, or verse that expresses the importance God places on relationships and the way you treat other people. Kindness is a particularly important trait, because it's one of those qualities that can be used to bless complete strangers—even in secrecy and anonymity. You can do kind things to people you don't know without them ever finding out who performed the act of kindness. As you use your time in kindness to others, you will also simplify your life by eliminating less productive activities.

Is someone in your church struggling to make ends meet? Ask your parents if you can put together a bag of groceries for the church to deliver to the family anonymously. Is a friend going through a rough time but isn't ready to talk about it? Send a card to let her know someone cares about what she's going through. You can show kindness in countless ways. Ask God to give you some ideas for how you can be a blessing through regular acts of kindness.

It's often said that kindness is contagious, and your own experience has probably proven that to be true. If someone lets you go in front of him in the lunch line one day, you are much more likely to do the same for a fellow classmate on the following day. Be proactive when it comes to kindness; be an example of kind and compassionate behavior to those around you. Most of all, let them see how the love of Christ permeates every kind act you perform.

## One Final Thought

Your positive actions will have positive consequences in the lives of others.

# *Thoughts for Simply Living*

Make every effort to add to your faith goodness; and to goodness, knowledge; and to knowledge, self-control; and to self-control, perseverance; and to perseverance, godliness; and to godliness, brotherly kindness; and to brotherly kindness, love.

2 PETER 1:5–7 NIV

The words of kindness are more healing to a drooping heart than balm or honey.

SARAH FIELDING

The fruit of the Spirit is love, joy, peace, patience, kindness, goodness, faithfulness, gentleness and self-control. Against such things there is no law.

GALATIANS 5:22–23 NIV

The greatest thing a man can do for his heavenly Father is to be kind to some of his other children.

HENRY DRUMMOND

# Remember...

_____In the hands of God's Spirit, even little acts of kindness can have major consequences.

_____Since kindness is contagious, you can help spread it around.

_____Anonymous acts of kindness often stem from pure motives, since there's no expectation of return.

_____Being kind requires so little, and yet it can change a person's day—or life.

## Simplify...

Write in your journal about how going the extra mile relates to kindness and how kindness, in turn, relates to simple living.

Ask God to give you creative ideas on how you can show kindness to others.

Do a Bible search for the words *kindness* and *compassion* to discover the importance God places on those qualities.

Choose one of the ideas God has given you and use it on someone.

This week, do one unusually kind thing for a family member—anonymously.

*The best portion of a good person's life is the little, nameless acts of kindness and love.*

WILLIAM WORDSWORTH

# Living Out Your Faith

In all things you yourself must be an example of good behavior.

Titus 2:7 GNT

What do your classmates see when they look at you? If your life is dedicated to pleasing and serving God, people will know it. Make no mistake about it: When people know you are a believer, they are watching you! They want to see if you live a life consistent with your faith—a joy-filled existence in which you trust God and treat other people well.

Throughout the Bible, God admonishes his people to be an example to those around them. In the Old Testament, the Lord wanted the Israelites' faith to show the surrounding cultures the power of God and the fruit of living a life consistent with his law. In the New Testament, God encouraged believers to serve as an example of godly freedom to the Jewish, Greek, and Roman cultures in which they lived. You can be sure that God wants you to do the same: Be an example of authentic Christian living—simple, honest, loving, faithful—for the culture in which you live.

Does that mean you have to be perfect? No. It means you

have to live in such a way that people see the victory you have in Christ as you go through the same struggles, problems, and difficulties that they experience. In witnessing your simple faith that God will see you through, they can experience the hope that the same faith is available to them as well.

Be transparent when it comes to your faith—live out your faith in an authentic way, telling what God has done for you, how God restores your faith when it begins to falter, even how God came through just when you were about to give up. People will appreciate your honesty and openness, and your example will enable them to see a real person with real struggles who has learned to rely on a real God.

Being an example is being yourself in the context of a life wholly devoted to God. Being an example is living a life consistent with what you believe. You need not worry about whether you are setting the right example as long as you are walking in obedience to him. Living your life honestly makes your life simpler because you don't have to hide, pretend, or decide what to do or say in tough situations.

## One Final Thought

A life of open faith in God can have a profound effect on your family, your friends, and your classmates.

# Thoughts for Simply Living

My life has been an example to many, because you have
been my strong defender. All day long I praise you and
proclaim your glory . . . I will always put my hope in you; I
will praise you more and more. I will tell of your goodness;
all day long I will speak of your salvation, though it is more
than I can understand.

PSALM 71:7–8, 14–15 GNT

The greatest gift we can bestow to others is a good example.

THOMAS MORELL

Follow my example, as I follow the example of Christ.

1 CORINTHIANS 11:1 NIV

There is only one influence that converts, and that is the example of a life
which is shot through and through with the glory and strength and
spirit of Christ.

HUGH RICHARD LAURIE SHEPPARD

# Remember...

_____People are always watching you, especially since you are a believer.

_____When people see you living an authentic Christian life, that life becomes more attractive to them.

_____As you walk in obedience to God, you become a good example to those around you.

_____People don't need to see a perfect Christian life—they need to see an honest one.

# Simplify...

Try to live every day in a manner that would encourage others to imitate you.

Ask God to show you how you can be a better example to others.

Think of someone you know whose life is "shot through and through" with Christ and choose to model that person.

Choose one way you can be an example of a joy-filled life and begin to live that way every day.

Write in your journal about how being a good example can simplify your life. Focus on the benefits of living a life consistent with what you believe.

_Have you noticed that when the shine is on your face and the ring is in your heart, this world will listen when you declare the praises of God?_

ROBERT E. COLEMAN

# Christian Companions

Anyone who walks with wise people grows wise.
Proverbs 13:20 NIrV

While there may be many people in your life that you call friends, you realize that that's just a convenient label; you know that only one or two people qualify as the kind of friend that you can entrust with your deepest feelings, allow to see your weaknesses, and count on to be there when you really need them. Trying to maintain too many friendships on that level is exhausting and futile. But a few good friends can keep you grounded and focused, simplifying your life immeasurably.

The Bible—particularly the book of Proverbs—offers frequent reminders about the importance of choosing your friends and companions carefully. It would be difficult, for example, to have a close friendship with someone who is not a believer, because the most important aspect of your life would be a mystery to him. Unwise friends complicate your life by tempting you to do things you shouldn't. They pull you into the things of the world and cause relational upheavals. So the Bible encourages you to find friends who are wise—that is, those who are believers like you—and who draw on the wisdom of God to direct their lives.

A believing friend offers so much more than one who has no understanding of the things of God. A believing friend is there to pray for your healing when you are sick, to pray for clarity of thought when you are upset or confused, and to pray for your faith to grow stronger. A believing friend can offer wisdom when you are going through a difficult time—or simply be there with you each step of the way. A believing friend can rejoice with you in your victories. And just as important, you can be there for her whenever she needs a friend.

In the coming years, you will be branching out and entering new environments—work, college, or the military—and you will be looking for new friends. Do yourself a favor and simplify your life by immediately connecting with Christians and with a church where you will find like-minded believers.

## One Final Thought

Friends who share your faith strengthen your faith and make it easier to live the life you choose.

# Thoughts for Simply Living

Happy are those who reject the advice of evil people, who do not follow the example of sinners or join those who have no use for God. Instead, they find joy in obeying the Law of the Lord, and they study it day and night. They are like trees that grow beside a stream, that bear fruit at the right time, and whose leaves do not dry up. They succeed in everything they do.

PSALM 1:1–3 GNT

From acquaintances, we conceal our real selves. To our friends we reveal our weaknesses.

BASIL HUME

Don't make friends with people who have hot, violent tempers. You might learn their habits and not be able to change.

PROVERBS 22:24 GNT

Inasmuch as any one pushes you nearer to God, he or she is your friend.

AUTHOR UNKNOWN

# Remember...

_____You can share things with a Christian friend that you can't share with an unbeliever.

_____Having one or two good friends is infinitely better than trying to develop close friendships with all of your acquaintances.

_____God wants you to choose your friends carefully to avoid ungodly influences.

_____To attract the right kind of friend, you must be the right kind of friend—a believer who shares in both the good and the bad times.

# Simplify...

Determine which of your friends draw you closer to God and work on relationships with them.

Ask God to show you which friends are unwise and how you should speak to them.

Ask God to help you be a good friend to someone who is in need of encouragement right now.

Resolve to be grounded and focused in such a way that your life becomes an encouragement for others.

Ask God to use you to strengthen the faith of one of your friends.

_If you want an accounting of your worth, count your friends._

MERRY BROWNE

# Straight to the Lord

I can do everything through him who gives me strength.
Philippians 4:13 NIV

As a believer, you should have an intense desire to do great things for God. You see kids in your school doing all the wrong things to gain acceptance, and you want them to know the acceptance you've found in God; your aunt and uncle are on the verge of separating, and you wish they would turn to God to save their marriage; your grandfather is bedridden and in pain, and it hurts you to see him suffer.

You want to believe that God will intervene, but sometimes it all seems so complicated. One speaker suggests you fast for a week; another promises an answer if you pray a certain prayer for a month; a third says God will not hear your prayers until you get rid of every last trace of sin in your life. Doesn't sound like the simple life you want, does it?

God does not expect you to jump through a series of religious hoops to get him to answer your prayers. Neither does he expect you to do great things for him in your own strength. What he wants is for you to let go of your religious effort and allow him to work through you. It's only through his power that you can accomplish "great things" anyway, and he is the only one who can answer your prayers.

Going straight to God will simplify your life. By doing so, you will be following the simple directives in his Word: Come to me, trust me, obey me, talk to me, listen to me, believe in me. Focus on studying the Bible to get the wisdom, strength, and direction you need.

Relying on God is the simplest and surest way to see him at work in your life and in the lives of others. Yes, you can learn from speakers and authors and other men and women of God. But spiritual power and ability and results come from God alone.

## One Final Thought

When you go straight to God, you can immediately access all that he has for you.

# Thoughts for Simply Living

The LORD is the one who keeps you safe. So let the Most
High God be like a home to you.

PSALM 91:9 NIrV

All God's giants have been weak men, who did great things for God
because they believed that God would be with them.

HUDSON TAYLOR

Trust in the LORD with all your heart and lean not on your
own understanding; in all your ways acknowledge him,
and he will make your paths straight.

PROVERBS 3:5–6 NIV

The very vastness of the work raises one's thoughts to God, as the only one
by whom it can be done. That is the solid comfort—he knows.

FLORENCE NIGHTINGALE

# Remember...

_____Faith allows you to go straight to God with those things in your life that you are concerned about.

_____When you depend on God, he can give you the strength and power to do great things in his name.

_____God wants to work through you, not through complicated religious maneuverings.

_____God wants simple trust and obedience from you when you rely on him.

## Simplify...

Meditate on both Philippians 4:13 and John 14:14. What does God as the source mean to you in a practical way?

Trust God with your most challenging prayer concerns.

Jeremiah was a teenager when God called him. Read Jeremiah 1 to see the level of trust he had in God and how it helped him.

Help a friend develop a deeper level of trust in God by sharing what you have learned about trusting him.

Consider how depending on God will simplify your quest to do great things.

*To make me forget my dependence on God is the devil's desire.*

SUSAN ANNETTE MUTO

# Giving Up the Struggle

Jesus said, "My grace is sufficient for you, for my power is made perfect in weakness." Therefore I will boast all the more gladly about my weaknesses, so that Christ's power may rest on me.

2 Corinthians 12:9 NIV

Few things can complicate your life as quickly and completely as perfectionism can. Perfectionism—the inability to accept anything that is less than perfect—drives people to either set ridiculously high standards for themselves and others or to give up altogether once they realize that perfection is unattainable. Either way, life as a perfectionist is far from simple, because the overachievers are in a constant struggle to do better and the underachievers are thoroughly dissatisfied with the turn their lives have taken.

But what does the Bible say about all this? Shouldn't believers make every effort to be perfect? Absolutely not. In the first place, the only one who is and ever will be perfect is God. In the second place, believers are to pursue excellence (Philippians 4:8 NRSV) not perfection. Even so, you need to be careful to keep your pursuit of excellence in the proper perspective. If you allow it to assume too important a place in your life, you will undoubtedly lose ground in your equally important pursuit of a simple life.

A perfectionistic approach to life results in worry, anxiety, failure, and a host of psychological problems like depression—not at all the kind of life God wants you to live. What's more, the excessive striving that accompanies perfectionism can lead to physical problems by weakening your immune system and making you more susceptible to illness. Your life as a believer suffers as you opt for working toward some unattainable spiritual goal instead of simply walking in obedience to the Lord. What God wants, though, is to see you learn to relax and trust in him as you continue to try to do your best.

Let go of perfectionism the minute you begin to recognize it in your life. Pursue excellence, but give up striving. Reduce the complications in your personal and academic life by setting realistic goals rather than unattainable ones. In so doing, you can simplify your life and get back to your purpose as a believer—to trust God in all that you attempt to accomplish in life.

## One Final Thought

Trusting God and trying your best can free you from the need to be perfect.

# Thoughts for Simply Living

I care very little if I am judged by you or by any human
court; indeed, I do not even judge myself.

1 CORINTHIANS 4:3 NIV

Demand perfection of yourself and you'll seldom attain it. Fear of making a
mistake is the biggest single cause of making one. Relax—pursue excellence,
not perfection.

BUD WINTER

I want to know Christ and the power of his resurrection
and the fellowship of sharing in his sufferings, becoming
like him in his death, and so, somehow, to attain to the
resurrection from the dead. Not that I have already obtained
all this, or have already been made perfect, but I press on to
take hold of that for which Christ Jesus took hold of me.

PHILIPPIANS 3:10–12 NIV

The plain truth is that there is no literal and absolute perfection among
true Christians, so long as they are in the body.

J. C. RYLE

# Remember...

_____Pursuing excellence is a far more profitable endeavor than striving for perfection.

_____When you rid yourself of perfectionism, your physical, emotional, and spiritual health will improve.

_____Your pursuit of a simple life will be more successful as you relax in the knowledge that God does not demand perfection from you.

_____God alone is perfect.

# Simplify...

When you set goals, make sure they are realistic and attainable.

As you notice perfectionist tendencies in yourself, deliberately choose to accept your flaws as evidence of your humanity.

Thank God for accepting you the way you are.

Give your struggle for perfection and your fear of failure to God.

Ask God to give you the grace to relax and trust him in all that you attempt to do.

*The thing that is really hard, and really amazing, is giving up on being perfect and beginning the work of being yourself.*

ANNA QUINDLEN

# Simple Living
## Spiritual Life

Faith is rest, not toil. It is the giving up of all the former weary efforts to do or feel something good, in order to induce God to love and pardon; and the calm reception of the truth that God loves and pardons of His own goodwill.

HORATIUS BONAR

*A heart at peace gives life to the body.*
PROVERBS 14:30 NIV

*Return to your rest, O my soul, for the LORD has dealt bountifully with you.*
PSALM 116:7 NASB

*But those who trust in the LORD for help will find their strength renewed. They will rise on wings like eagles; they will run and not get weary; they will walk and not grow weak.*
ISAIAH 40:31 GNT

It's simple, really.

"There is only one thing needful"—

To sit at the feet of Jesus.

And yet so easily we're turned aside

By things that matter less—

By things that matter not at all.

We bend beneath the weight of burdens

We were never asked to bear.

We fill our lives so full

We cannot hear the voice

Of Him who loves us,

Who whispers to our weary souls,

"Come to me, and I will give you rest."

W. Marvin Hardy

# One Ambition

We also have as our ambition, whether at home or absent,
to be pleasing to him.

2 Corinthians 5:9 NASB

What are your ambitions—making the honor roll? getting into an Ivy League school? becoming a millionaire? People are motivated by many different ambitions. The apostle Paul said you should have just one ambition: to be pleasing to God. But what about school, and what about the future? How can you expect to get anywhere in life if you don't have ambitions? Jesus answered those questions. "Seek first [God's] kingdom and his righteousness, and all these things will be given to you as well" (Matthew 6:33 NIV).

The pursuit of God is the only ambition that carries the promise that you can "have it all." Seek first that which is truly first, and then watch everything else fall into place. That doesn't necessarily mean you'll get rich or get into a big-name school. But it does mean that you will have what you hoped to gain through those other ambitions—joy, security, satisfaction, and meaning. Viewing things from an eternal perspective also serves to motivate you to work hard at school, work, relationships, and all the other important aspects of your life. An eternal perspective gives you the ability to see what is genuinely important. The essence of simple living is to devote your first energies to that which matters most. Having one ambition simplifies your life by allowing you to sort out the trivial and unimportant things that detract from your larger goals.

Grades provide a good example of how the pursuit of godliness can displace worldly ambitions. Try viewing your education from an eternal perspective. Your mind—your ability to learn, to understand, to reason, to solve problems—is created in the image of God. As you exercise your mind by reading a poem or unraveling an algebra problem, you're growing in the image of God. Such a perspective teaches you to love learning and appreciate what's beautiful and orderly about the world you're studying. With that kind of attitude, you can be sure that your grades will take care of themselves.

Make it your ambition to please God. No other ambition offers such a sure guarantee of success. If you seek God you will find him, and he will give you the desires of your heart.

## One Final Thought

Your ambitions shape your priorities, and your priorities shape your life.

# Thoughts for Simply Living

[We ask] God to fill you with the knowledge of his will through all spiritual wisdom and understanding. And we pray this in order that you may live a life worthy of the Lord and may please him in every way: bearing fruit in every good work, growing in the knowledge of God, being strengthened with all power.

COLOSSIANS 1:9–11 NIV

Do not let it be your aim to be something, but to be someone.

VICTOR HUGO

Don't do anything from selfish ambition or from a cheap desire to boast.

PHILIPPIANS 2:3 GNT

Unless you know what you want, you can't ask for it.

JEANNE SEGAL

# Remember...

_____Focus on what you truly value, not on the things you think will get you what you truly value.

_____When you are motivated by a desire to please God, everything else has a way of working itself out.

_____It's not just your performance that pleases God. Your pleasure also pleases him.

_____When you view your work as a service to God, you'll find joy in doing your best.

# Simplify...

Make a list of your ambitions. Do any of them hinder the pursuit of godliness?

Make yourself accountable to a godly friend who can help keep your priorities in line.

Decide where your talents lie, and focus your efforts there.

Do your personal best for God's glory.

Connect with others who share your ambition to please God.

_No lions are ever caught in mousetraps._

THOMAS DREIER

147

# A Still, Small Voice

Everyone should be quick to listen, slow to speak, and slow to become angry.
James 1:19 NIV

Picture the prophet Elijah standing on a mountaintop. God promised to pass by that place, and Elijah was waiting to see him. A terrifying wind howled through, sending pieces of rock flying. But God wasn't in the wind. An earthquake shook the mountain all the way to its base. But God wasn't in the earthquake. A fire appeared, and Elijah had to shield his face from its crackling, popping intensity. But God wasn't in the fire. Then Elijah heard a whisper, and he knew that God was speaking. The wind, the fire, and the earthquake all demanded the prophet's attention. But to hear God, Elijah had to listen.

Are you able to listen for what is true and important? Your life can get so filled up with things that seem momentous—winds, earthquakes, fires, term papers, concerts, big games—that you can't hear what matters even more—the stirrings of God's Spirit or the quiet cry of a friend in need. To hear those things, you have to make a conscious effort. You have to carve out time to reflect, time to read and pray, time to listen to friends and family. You have to turn off the television, turn down the radio, and focus on what's being said. This simplifies life by keeping you from wasting energy, time, and words.

It isn't just outside distractions that make it hard to listen. Sometimes you can't hear for the sound of your own voice. It's hard to hear what another person is trying to communicate when you're busy talking or thinking about what you're going to say next. So slow down. Listen. If you understand first before you try to make yourself understood, you'll be amazed at your ability to communicate your point of view. And you'll be able to hear more than simply the words that another person is speaking. You'll be able to hear the truth.

There's always something screaming for your attention—some emergency, some deadline, some conflict, some television show or ball game. The things that are truest and most important, however, often don't scream at you. They whisper. They wait until you're ready to listen.

## One Final Thought

If you want to learn how to listen to God,
you can start by learning to listen to other people.

# Thoughts for Simply Living

Jesus said, "My sheep listen to my voice; I know them, and they follow me."

JOHN 10:27 NIV

We need to find God, and he cannot be found in noise and restlessness. God is the friend of silence. See how nature—trees, flowers, grass— grows in silence; see the stars, the moon and the sun, how they move in silence . . . We need silence to be able to touch souls.

MOTHER TERESA

When words are many, sin is not absent, but he who holds his tongue is wise.

PROVERBS 10:19 NIV

To talk without thinking is to shoot without aiming.

ENGLISH PROVERB

# Remember...

_____A good listener is a good friend.

_____Things that shout for your attention may not be as important as they seem.

_____When you think there's a lot you need to say, you can be sure there's even more you need to hear.

_____If you're looking for the wisest people, look for the ones who are asking questions.

# Simplify...

When you're being introduced to another person, focus on that person's name instead of on what you're going to say so that you can avoid the struggle later to remember.

Turn off the car radio. Car time can be good time for listening to God or others.

The first thing out of your mouth is rarely the wisest. Think twice, speak once, and you won't have to retract your words later.

Ask God to help you hear his voice so you'll know what is true and important.

When stray thoughts interrupt your prayers, write them down and return to them later.

_The Hebrew word in the Old Testament usually translated "to understand" also means "to listen."_

HAROLD SALA

# Are You Good-Looking Enough?

Your beauty should consist of your true inner self, the ageless beauty of a gentle and quiet spirit, which is of the greatest value in God's sight.
1 Peter 3:4 GNT

You've probably had the dream where you're sitting in class and suddenly realize that you aren't fully dressed or you forgot to comb your hair or put on your makeup. Almost everybody has that dream. The thought of facing the world when you're not looking your best is the stuff of nightmares.

The way others perceive you affects your self-image. That's an unavoidable part of being human. The important thing is to be sure that the perceptions of others—especially their perceptions of your appearance—don't determine your self-image. Does a new pimple ruin your day? Do you get up two hours early just so you can make it through your morning routine? Do you spend more time looking in the bathroom mirror than looking into God's Word? The point, of course, isn't to stop showering or combing your hair or cleaning the wax out of your ears. God gave you a body, and you should take care of it. A key principle of simple living, however, is allotting your time and energy according to what's most important. There's a lot more to you than your looks.

When it comes to personal appearance, everybody has a distinct style. You prefer a certain kind of clothes; you've chosen to fix your hair a certain way; you may wear makeup a particular way. But ask yourself this: does your style express your true self or does your style conceal your true self? Some teens hide behind conformity. Others hide behind a style so outrageous that nobody can see through to the real person. It's a lot simpler just to be yourself. Outer beauty may be only skin-deep, but inner beauty—a confident, compassionate, content, complete self—is going to shine through to the outside. Believe it or not, the real you, the one made in the image of God, is more attractive than any facade you can put on.

Are you good-looking enough? You sure are. You are the person God made, the person God is continuing to perfect day by day. So peel away any layers you put on to hide from others, and settle on a personal style that's you and not somebody else.

## One Final Thought

Your friends are a lot more interested in what you have inside than how you look on the surface.

# Thoughts for Simply Living

The LORD does not look at the things man looks at. Man looks at the outer appearance, but the LORD looks at the heart.

1 SAMUEL 16:7 NIV

Is the jay more precious than the lark because his feathers are more beautiful? Or is the adder better than the eel because his painted skin contents the eye?

WILLIAM SHAKESPEARE

Charm is deceptive, and beauty is fleeting; but a woman who fears the LORD is to be praised.

PROVERBS 31:30 NIV

Beauty is no beauty without love.

THOMAS CAMPION

# Remember...

_____One way to start appreciating your own inner beauty is to appreciate it in others. When you look at other people, look past the surface.

_____Genuine style is about showing the real you; it's not about chasing the latest fad.

_____The things you might hope to gain through good looks—acceptance, security, love—are given freely and fully by the God who loves you more than you love yourself.

_____Even self-consciousness can be a kind of selfishness. If you're overly concerned about your looks, your coolness, your ability to fit in, you can't be overly concerned about other people.

## Simplify...

Think through your grooming routine, and trim away any steps that are redundant or unnecessary.

Meditate on Christ and his love to develop inner beauty.

Get honest about your attitude toward looks. List the benefits of good looks. Are they genuine benefits?

Read through the Fruits of the Spirit (Galatians 5: 22–23). This is genuine beauty.

Try to spend more time cultivating your inner life than you spend on your outward appearance.

*Beauty lurks where you least expect to find it.*

JON MARANS

# Are Your Relatives as Crazy as Mine?

What are relatives for if not to share trouble?
Proverbs 17:17 GNT

You want to simplify your life, but if there's one area of life that never seems simple, it's family. Most families appear to be a raucous mass of sibling rivalry, horseplay, fierce loyalties, little rebellions, and schedule conflicts. How can that be simple?

Truth is, living with your family probably won't ever be simple. But it's worth the trouble. Simple living doesn't mean every aspect of your life has to be simple. It means you simplify where you can so you have more time and energy to invest where it matters most—in family, for instance.

Even if you can't hope for simplicity in your family life, though, there are ways you can make things less complicated. Conflict inevitably arises in families, just as it does in all human relationships. The apostle Paul gave some good advice for keeping the peace: "If it is possible, as far as it depends on you, live at peace with everyone" (Romans

12:18 NIV). Paul instructed Christians to do more than their share. That may sound hard; but doing more than your share to keep the peace is a lot simpler than keeping up your end of a feud! Paul was careful to say "as far as it depends on you," because it doesn't all depend on one person. If the other party to a conflict refuses to make peace, you may be unable to do anything about it. Chances are, however, if you go the extra mile to make peace, your family members will meet you there.

If sibling rivalry seems unavoidable in your family, let it be a rivalry to see who can be the most forgiving, the most understanding, or the most loving. If you feel your parents don't understand who you are or what you're going through, give them the benefit of the doubt. They probably understand a lot more than you think they do.

Family life may at times be stormy. Nevertheless, family life is a shelter from the larger storms that rage outside. Family life may never be simple, and yet it is always worth the trouble.

## One Final Thought

Other relationships come and go, but your family is your family forever.

# Thoughts for Simply Living

Love one another, and be kind and humble with one another.

1 Peter 3:8 GNT

A family in harmony will prosper in everything.

Ancient Proverb

It is your Christian duty to obey your parents, for this is the right thing to do. "Respect your father and mother" is the first commandment that has a promise added: "so that all may go well with you, and you may live a long time in the land."

Ephesians 6:1–3 GNT

Birds in their little nests agree; and 'tis a shameful sight when children of one family fall out, and chide, and fight.

Isaac Watts

# Remember...

_____Be patient and forgiving of your parents.

_____The love between family members is unique among human relationships.

_____The Bible describes the people of God as a family. Learning to live joyfully among your earthly family is good practice for your membership in the family of God.

_____Living simply in all aspects of your life leaves more time and energy for the complex business of family life.

# Simplify...

Make it a point to be the first to make peace, whether you are right or wrong.

Ask God to heal any resentment between you and other family members.

Tell your family that you love them. They need to hear you say it.

Be kind to your siblings, especially younger siblings.

Do more than your share around the house. Initiative is contagious.

*In the end, it will be the family way of life that will persevere.*

MARGARET MEAD

# Tomorrow, Tomorrow

Let us not become tired of doing good; for if we do not give up, the time will come when we will reap the harvest.

Galatians 6:9 GNT

Procrastination is a most deceptive habit. When you put something off, it feels like you have some control over your situation. "Sure," you say to yourself, "those teachers can pile all this work on me, but I'm not going to do it until I'm good and ready." In fact, however, you've forfeited control. The deadline eventually comes barreling down on you, and you have no choice but to hunker down and do the work. Now all control, all choice, is gone.

The assignment owns you. A friend calls to see if you want to hit some tennis balls. Too bad. You've got work to do. Your favorite TV show is on tonight. Too bad. You've got work to do. Bedtime comes and goes, and you're starting to feel sleepy. Too bad. You've got work to do. To your surprise, you start getting interested in something from the assigned reading and wish you could dig a little deeper. Too bad. You've got work to do. So you work twice as hard, endure twice as much stress, and turn in work that's half as good as it would have been if you had done your work in a timely manner.

Urgency is a hard master. When you procrastinate, you choose not to govern yourself through discipline, and choose instead to let urgency govern you. Urgency isn't the same thing as importance. Many of the most important things in your life—especially relationships—rarely seem urgent. If you are motivated only by urgency, less urgent things—the unimportant things and the important things too—start to fall by the wayside.

How do you stop procrastinating? Face up to the real reason you're putting off your work. Is it a fear of failure? Defiance of the authorities who tell you what to do? Uncertainty about how to do the work? Pride that prevents you from asking for the help you need to get started? Just plain laziness? Whatever is at the root of your procrastination, pray through it. Repent, and ask God to release you. Then do something.

## One Final Thought

Starting a task you've been putting off is like getting into a cold pool. It's best just to jump straight in; soon you realize it's not so bad.

# Thoughts for Simply Living

Suppose you have something to give. Don't say to your
neighbor, "Come back later. I'll give it to you tomorrow."
PROVERBS 3:28 NIrV

Don't put things on the back burner; they might fall off the stove.
PHILLIP H. BARNHART

A farmer too lazy to plow his fields at the right time
will have nothing to harvest.
PROVERBS 20:4 GNT

Don't worry about being slow; just worry about stopping.
ANCIENT PROVERB

# Remember...

_____Now is always the best time to do what's right.

_____Taking control of your time is difficult enough under the best circumstances. When you procrastinate, you find that your deadlines take control of you.

_____Diligence in your day-to-day tasks trains your mind and heart for diligence in things of eternal importance.

_____When you procrastinate, even easy tasks become hard.

# Simplify...

Keep a list of the things you need to do each day, and refer to it throughout the day.

What three items on your to-do list do you dread the most? Do those things first.

Don't ask, "Do I feel like starting on this?" Ask, "Is it time to get started?"

Set and meet deadlines for yourself that are earlier than the deadlines imposed by others.

If you're working on a computer, disable your Internet connection (especially instant messaging) until you're finished.

_Procrastination is the thief of time._

EDWARD YOUNG

# Simple Living
## Relationships

*Two are better than one, because they have a good return for their work; if one falls down, his friend can help him up. But pity the man who falls and has no one to help him up!*

ECCLESIASTES 4:9–10 NIV

The greatest sweetener of human life is Friendship.

JOSEPH ADDISON

*People learn from one another, just as iron sharpens iron.*

PROVERBS 27:17 GNT

*Jesus replied, "The most important [command] is this: 'Listen, Israel! The Lord our God is the only Lord. Love the Lord your God with all your heart, with all your soul, with all your mind, and with all your strength.' The second most important commandment is this: 'Love your neighbor as you love yourself.' There is no other commandment more important than these two."*

MARK 12:29–31 GNT

People are never simple.

It's no simple matter

To love your neighbor as yourself,

No simple matter

To treat others as you would be treated.

But what could be more important?

The simple life has just one goal:

To make room for the things that matter—

Room for friends and loved ones

Who, however complicated they may seem,

Ask very simple things:

"Hear me." "Love me." "Walk beside me."

SHARON K. ALLSBROOK

# Romeo! Juliet!

*My God will meet all your needs according to his glorious riches in Christ Jesus.*
Philippians 4:19 NIV

You know that famous scene from Romeo and Juliet—the one where Juliet is standing on her balcony and Romeo is in the garden below. They have only known each other for a few hours at that point; they met at a party earlier the same night. Juliet is sighing and cooing over her lover. Romeo is promising his eternal love to Juliet. They're just two teenagers, but they have each other, and that makes them complete. They see a future of unfailing devotion and perfect happiness stretching out before them.

Romeo and Juliet are held up as the ideal lovers in all of English literature. That's probably because their story was finished long before reality set in. They were still in the first bloom of infatuation when they met their sad end. And yet, as unrealistic as their story was, do you secretly want to be Romeo or Juliet? Do you want to meet somebody you can love with an overpowering love, who'll love you back the same way? Somebody who will complete you?

Here's the problem: there isn't anybody out there who will complete you. It's God's job to make you whole, and not anybody else's. You've known people who felt they had to be in a dating relationship at all times—people who would rather have a boyfriend or girlfriend who made them miserable than not have a boyfriend or girlfriend at all. The desire for romance can be exhausting, a real drain on your mental and emotional reserves (and sometimes your cash reserves).

Dating isn't a bad thing. You can have a lot of fun dating. You can learn a lot about yourself, and there's a good chance you'll get to know your future spouse through dating. But if you're pinning all your hopes for happiness on one person—or on the expectation of meeting that one person—you're asking for trouble. Simply live, and don't expect a dating relationship to fulfill your deepest desires. Those are fulfilled by the God who promises to supply your every need. When it's time, he'll bring the right person into your life. It's the simplest way.

## One Final Thought

No relationship with a person can fully satisfy—only a relationship with God can do that.

# Thoughts for Simply Living

I pray that you may have your roots and foundation in love,
so that you, together with all God's people, may have the
power to understand how broad and long, how high and
deep, is Christ's love. Yes, may you come to know his love—
although it can never be fully known—and so be completely
filled with the very nature of God.

EPHESIANS 3:17–19 GNT

Who God possesseth in nothing is wanting; alone God sufficeth.

SAINT THERESA OF AVILA

He guides the humble in what is right and teaches them his
way. All the ways of the LORD are loving and faithful for
those who keep the demands of his covenant.

PSALM 25:9–10 NIV

Romance is tempestuous. Love is calm.

MASON COOLEY

# Remember...

_____Friends of your own gender are good choices to hold you accountable to biblical standards in your dating.

_____When you're feeling lonely or insecure, you can turn to God for comfort.

_____God's timing is perfect. When it's time for you to have a serious relationship, God will bring that person to you.

_____It's easier to set emotional and physical boundaries early in a dating relationship, when things are relatively casual.

## Simplify...

Consider arranging a group date with other friends rather than pairing off with one person so that you spare yourself undue pressure.

Ask God to help you be content in his all-sufficient love.

List the most important qualities you seek in a boyfriend or girlfriend so that you don't settle for someone who is unsuitable for you.

Pray that God will bring your future spouse into your life when the time is right.

For a first date, go for ice cream or coffee, something casual and noncommittal,

_True love comes quietly, without banners or flashing lights._
_If you hear bells, get your ears checked._

ERICH SEGAL

169

# Go for the Gold

Every athlete in training submits to strict discipline, in order to be crowned with a wreath that will not last; but we do it for one that will last forever.

1 Corinthians 9:25 GNT

In the movie *Chariots of Fire*, the missionary and Olympic runner Eric Liddell had an intense conversation with his sister Jenny. She was concerned that his commitment to sports had begun to overshadow his greater purpose of missionary work in China. "Jenny, Jenny," Eric answered, "you've got to understand. I believe God made me for a purpose—for China. But he also made me fast. And when I run, I feel his pleasure!" As Eric Liddell demonstrated, a truly "spiritual" person pays attention to more than just the spirit. God also gave you a body to cultivate and to use to his glory. Sports are a great way to develop the physical part of your personhood.

Training for sports develops habits of mind that serve you well in all aspects of your life. When you train with a team, you learn the value of playing through pain and of willing yourself through temporary hardship for the rewards of victory later. You learn the importance of delayed gratification.

Equally valuable is the simple pleasure of pushing your body beyond what is easy or comfortable, and learning that you can do things that you didn't know you could do. Stretching your legs, raising your heart rate, feeling yourself grow stronger, you get the feeling of being more alive, a more complete person. As you feel the pleasure of training and competition, you feel God's pleasure in you.

Physical activity can help you to be more productive in other activities, but it is important not to pursue sports so much that they complicate your life. As hard as he trained for the Olympic team, Eric Liddell kept his running in eternal perspective. Soon after he set the world record for the 400-meter race, he rejoined his family on the mission field in China. There he spent the rest of his life preaching, teaching, coaching, and, on occasion, racing. He was training to win a victor's crown even greater than his Olympic gold medal.

## One Final Thought

Your highest purpose is to glorify God and enjoy him forever. Sports provide you the opportunity to do both.

# Thoughts for Simply Living

I have fought the good fight, I have finished the race, I have kept the faith. Now there is in store for me the crown of righteousness, which the Lord, the righteous Judge, will award to me on that day—and not only to me, but also to all who have longed for his appearing.

2 TIMOTHY 4:7–8 NIV

The bow cannot always stand bent, nor can human frailty subsist without some lawful recreation.

MIGUEL DE CERVANTES

I harden my body with blows and bring it under complete control, to keep myself from being disqualified after having called others to the contest.

1 CORINTHIANS 9:27 GNT

Mens sana in corpore sano: "A healthy mind in a healthy body."

ANCIENT LATIN PHRASE

# Remember...

_____The training you do for sports is good training for every other aspect of your life.

_____God gave you your body. Running, jumping, and playing a sport that interests can help keep your body in shape for God's service.

_____You can make important contributions to the team even if you aren't the star player.

_____Playing sports is a great way to get involved in the lives of people who aren't in your usual social crowd. You can have an impact on them by showing integrity, sportsmanship, and an encouraging spirit.

## Simplify...

If you want to improve, compete against people who play a little better than you do.

Training in the off-season makes in-season training go a lot better.

Injuries from overtraining can be a real setback. Take care of yourself as you train.

Learn to play smarter, not just harder.

A good diet, including plenty of water, is an important part of a sports training regimen.

_I was nervous, so I read the New Testament. I read the verse about have no fear, and I felt relaxed. Then I jumped farther than I ever jumped before in my life._

WILLYE WHITE, U.S. 1956 OLYMPIC SILVER MEDALIST, WOMAN'S LONG JUMP

# Taste and See—the Lord is Good

Food, however, will not improve our relation with God; we shall not lose anything if we do not eat, nor shall we gain anything if we do eat.

1 Corinthians 8:8 GNT

Have you ever eaten a bowl of ice cream (or two) to make yourself feel better after a hard day at school? Do you drink a caffeinated soft drink to boost your energy? Do you swing by the drive-through or stop at the vending machine for a quick bite before a rehearsal or a club meeting instead of eating a balanced meal? Sometimes food or drink can be a quick fix for a short-term problem. But the ill effects of too much junk food, fast food, sweets, or caffeine can last a long time.

Eating right is a crucial part of a balanced, simplified lifestyle. You'll have less sickness, more energy, and better mental sharpness if you eat a good diet with plenty of fresh vegetables and fruits, lots of water, and as little processed sugar, fast food, junk food, and caffeine as possible. Basing your food choices on nutritional value, and not just on how food makes you feel at the moment, pays long-term dividends.

Remember, however, that no diet is going to solve all your problems, in spite of what the diet books say. Some people take strict control of their diet because they feel out of control in other aspects of their lives. They practice grueling eating habits as a kind of self-discipline. But the enjoyment you get from eating is a gift from God. Self-deprivation for its own sake doesn't honor him.

The Bible provides lots of advice about eating. But it also makes it clear that you have freedom. Eat healthfully. Take care of yourself. Don't get uptight about food. Consider this: God didn't have to make food taste good. If God had so chosen, he could have made a gray mush containing every nutrient human beings need. Gray mush for breakfast. Gray mush for lunch. Gray mush for dinner. Same thing tomorrow. And the next day. It would have served the purpose. But instead he made oranges, sweet peas, steak, wheat, broccoli, honey—a whole world of marvelous things to eat. Taste and see that the Lord is good.

## One Final Thought

God is a giver of good gifts. One of his best gifts is food. It strengthens your body, gives you pleasure, and provides the chance to fellowship with friends and family.

# Thoughts for Simply Living

"They will rejoice in the bounty of the LORD—the grain, the new wine and the oil, the young of the flocks and herds. They will be like a well-watered garden, and they will sorrow no more . . . I will satisfy the priests with abundance, and my people will be filled with my bounty," declares the LORD.

JEREMIAH 31:12, 14 NIV

Tell me what you eat, and I will tell you what you are.

ANTHELME BRILLAT-SAVARIN

Whether you eat or drink or whatever you do, do it all for the glory of God.

1 CORINTHIANS 10:31 NIV

Eat less when you dine; live to age ninety-nine.

ANCIENT PROVERB

# Remember...

_____Good food is a reminder that God provides for your every need abundantly.

_____Like all of God's gifts, food is best enjoyed in moderation. Too much food, or the wrong balance of foods, becomes harmful rather than pleasurable.

_____When you feel lonely or sad, it is better to turn to the God who meets every need and to avoid junk food and sweets.

_____You're always in God's hands, and you can enjoy his blessings.

# Simplify...

Eat with small bites and chew slowly. Enjoy every mouthful in a relaxed frame of mind.

If you have after-school activities, bring healthy snacks so you can resist a junk-food fix.

Thank God for every meal. Saying grace isn't just a ritual. It's an acknowledgment that God sustains you and provides healthy nutrients.

If you have a sweet tooth, keep a bag of baby carrots on hand for snacks.

Cook a meal for your family or friends. Cooking for another person is an act of service that puts the focus away from you.

_Some people have food and no appetite. Some people have appetite and no food. Thank you, Lord, that I have both._

OLD ENGLISH PRAYER

# Don't Look Down

God hath not given us the spirit of fear; but of power, and of love,
and of a sound mind.

2 Timothy 1:7 KJV

Everybody knows about Jesus walking on the water. Do
you remember that Peter walked on water too? When he
saw Jesus coming across the lake, he jumped out of his boat
and walked toward him. Buoyed by his faith and by the love
of his master, Peter wasn't subject even to the laws of gravity.
But then he saw the wind and the waves. He remembered
that a man can't walk on water, and he was frightened.
Thinking he should get a better look at the mess he had
gotten himself in, he took his eyes off Jesus. That's when he
began to sink.

Fear can make you flounder in the water instead of
cruising across the surface. Fear can make you sink.

What's the opposite of fear? Power. Love. Sound
judgment.

As you turn your fears over to the God who loves you

and upholds you, he gives you the power to live a life that pleases him. You can stop thrashing about. You don't have to try to conquer your fears in your own strength (and wear yourself out in the process). To those who seek his face, God grants a spirit of power—power to love others, power to do what's right even in difficult situations, power to make good decisions, and power to be joyful.

As you turn your fears over to God, you tap into his power that allows you to reach beyond whatever fear may threaten you. His power can sharpen your vision and enable you to see the way out of your dilemma. God's grace and mercy will deliver you from your failures and make you bold in his love. You'll be able to resist negative peer pressure and to fight temptations of all sorts. Just keep your eyes on Jesus.

## One Final Thought

It's hard to be afraid when you're looking into the face of God.

# Thoughts for Simply Living

Those who are led by God's Spirit are God's children. For the Spirit that God has given you does not make you slaves and cause you to be afraid; instead, the Spirit makes you God's children, and by the Spirit's power we cry out to God, "Father! my Father!" God's Spirit joins himself to our spirits to declare that we are God's children.

ROMANS 8:14–16, GNT

Courage is fear that has said its prayers.

DOROTHY BERNARD

It was for freedom that Christ set us free; therefore keep standing firm and do not be subject again to a yoke of slavery.

GALATIANS 5:1 NASB

The spirit of love to God will set us above the fear of man, and all the hurt that a man can do us.

MATTHEW HENRY

# Remember...

_____This is God's world. He is always on the throne of his universe.

_____Your confidence is founded on the strength of God, in whom you've placed your faith. Your faithfulness is sometimes stronger, sometimes weaker, but God is perfectly faithful.

_____Fear complicates life, but God is on your side.

_____The key to courage is remembering. Remember what a great and faithful God has promised to uphold and protect you.

# Simplify...

God gives you a spirit of power. Pray for wisdom to use that power to God's glory.

> List the ways God has delivered you in the past. When you're afraid, read this list.

Tap into God's power and reach beyond your fear.

> Dwell on the fact that God has a perfect plan for your future.

Resist temptation by keeping your eyes on Jesus.

*The key to success is for you to make a habit throughout your life of doing the things you fear.*

BRIAN TRACY

181

# Don't Forget to Breathe

There is an appointed time for everything. And there is a time for every event under heaven.

Ecclesiastes 3:1 NASB

What if you had to remember to breathe? "Breathe in . . . breathe out . . . breathe in . . ." And don't forget to make your heart beat. "Breathe in . . . beat . . . breathe out . . . beat . . . breathe in . . . beat . . ." You'd never get anything done. Thankfully, your body has involuntary functions that take care of these functions without your thinking about them—so you can do other things besides sitting around breathing and beating your heart.

Routines are to your daily life what involuntary functions are to your body. A routine enables you to accomplish things without really thinking about them. When you get dressed in the morning, you don't consciously decide whether to put on your shoes or your socks first. It's socks first, then shoes. That's the routine. The tiny bit of mental energy you saved there can be used to decide whether you need to wear a sweater or a jacket. Or better yet, if you picked out your sweater as part of your bedtime routine the night before, there's one thing off your list for the hectic morning time. It may seem like a small thing, but as you fit more and more of your daily tasks into routines that you don't have to think about, the savings of time and energy can add up to a saner, more relaxed, and more focused life.

Routines aren't just about saving time and energy. A good daily plan helps make sure the most important things—and not just the most urgent things—get done every day. Take prayer and Scripture reading, for instance. You probably agree that they are important. But if praying and Scripture reading aren't part of your daily routine, like brushing your teeth or putting on your shoes, they'll be the first things you drop when things get busy. What else is important to you? Make those things part of your schedule so you can be sure they get done.

A word of warning about routines: your routine exists to serve you; you don't exist to serve the routine. So be flexible. Things come up that are more important than even the best-planned routine. But without a plan, you have no way of judging which activities are worth your time and which aren't.

## One Final Thought

The structure provided by a good schedule helps you protect one of your most valuable assets: your time.

# Thoughts for Simply Living

Jesus said, "Seek first his kingdom and his righteousness, and all these things will be added to you as well. Therefore, do not worry about tomorrow, for tomorrow will worry about itself. Each day has enough trouble of its own."

MATTHEW 6:33–34 NIV

How we spend our days is, of course, how we spend our lives.

ANNIE DILLARD

Plan carefully what you do, and whatever you do will turn out right.

PROVERBS 4:26 GNT

To know that which before us lies in daily life is the prime wisdom.

JOHN MILTON

# Remember...

_____Having a good routine for the little tasks of everyday life leaves you more time and energy to tackle the bigger tasks.

_____A routine is as individual as the person who keeps it.

_____The key to an effective daily plan is putting first things first. An established schedule protects you from the urgent things that are always barging in on the important things.

_____God is a God of order. When you get your life in order, you're reflecting the image of God.

# Simplify...

Decide what matters most to you, and anchor your daily routine around those activities.

Every day, set aside time to plan. Make daily planning part of your daily plan.

Consider long-term goals in your daily schedule. Each day, make a little progress toward your goals.

Make sure daily downtime is part of the plan.

Break big projects into manageable steps that can be incorporated into your routine.

_The only way to live is to accept each minute as an unrepeatable miracle, which is exactly what it is—a miracle and unrepeatable._

MARGARET STORM JAMESON

# Simple Living School

Do you see a man skilled in his work? He will serve before kings; he will not serve before obscure men.

PROVERBS 22:29 NIV

The highest reward that God gives us for good work is the ability to do better work.

ELBERT HUBBARD

Whatever your hand finds to do, do it with all your might.

ECCLESIASTES 9:10 NASB

Commit to the LORD whatever you do, and your plans will succeed.

PROVERBS 16:3 NIV

Lord God of algebra,

Lord God of gym class,

Lord God of dishwashing:

You are the Lord of all things.

In You all things hold together.

I am one person.

I prefer to live one life,

In service to the One God

Who fills every task

With sacredness.

ANDREW H. IVESTER

When you live intentionally, you automatically slow down and become more receptive to God speaking to you.

Everything that happens in this world happens at the time God chooses.

ECCLESIASTES 3:1 NIV

Your pursuit of a simple life will be more successful as you relax in the knowledge that God does not demand perfection from you.

At Inspirio we love to hear from you—your
stories, your feedback,
and your product ideas.
Please send your comments to us
by way of e-mail at
icares@zondervan.com
or to the address below:

**inspirio**

Attn: Inspirio Cares
5300 Patterson Avenue SE
Grand Rapids, MI 49530

If you would like further information
about Inspirio and the products we
create, please visit us at:
www.inspiriogifts.com

Thank you and God Bless!